Empirical Analysis of Poverty Dynamics

**Göttinger Studien zur Entwicklungsökonomik**
**Göttingen Studies in Development Economics**
Herausgegeben von/ Edited by Hermann Sautter und/and Stephan Klasen

Bd./Vol. 21

PETER LANG
Frankfurt am Main · Berlin · Bern · Bruxelles · New York · Oxford · Wien

Isabel Günther

# Empirical Analysis of Poverty Dynamics

## With Case Studies from Sub-Saharan Africa

PETER LANG
Internationaler Verlag der Wissenschaften

**Bibliographic Information published by the Deutsche Nationalbibliothek**
The Deutsche Nationalbibliothek lists this publication in the Deutsche Nationalbibliografie; detailed bibliographic data is available in the internet at <http://www.d-nb.de>.

Zugl.: Göttingen, Univ., Diss., 2007

Gratefully acknowledging the support of the
Ibero-Amerika-Institut für Wirtschaftsforschung, Göttingen.

Cover illustration by courtesy of the
Ibero-Amerika-Institut für Wirtschaftsforschung, Göttingen.

D 7
ISSN 1439-3395
ISBN 978-3-631-57373-0



www.peterlang.de

to Viola

# Editor's Preface

Despite an extensive literature on defining and measuring poverty, the dimension time has until recently somewhat been neglected. However, time or poverty dynamics are certainly important for an appropriate understanding of individuals' current as well as lifetime wellbeing. Time does not only allow for a distinction between permanent and temporary poverty but also for an incorporation of the notion of (poverty-) risk in wellbeing analysis, which is of high relevance if we assume that individuals are risk-averse. Moreover, closely related to poverty dynamics is an analysis of the causes of poverty: With static measurements, i.e. without a time dimensions, one cannot go beyond an analysis of the correlates of poverty. Analysis of poverty dynamics, hence, also makes it possible to better understand the causes of poverty. The empirical application of the concept of poverty dynamics is, however, still severely constrained by data limitations. In the past, these data limitations have often been assumed away, which might have led to biased assessments of poverty dynamics as well as to a neglect of certain aspects of poverty dynamics.

This present book entitled *Empirical Analysis of Poverty Dynamics* is built on four essays which analyze different aspects of poverty dynamics, where Isabel Günther explicitly takes into account existing data limitations and proposes alternative methods to analyze poverty over time. The proposed methods are applied to household survey data from various sub-Saharan African countries. The first two essays of the book discuss difficulties related to limited data in the analysis of macro-level (or national) poverty dynamics whereas the last two essays discuss difficulties related to missing data in the analysis of micro-level poverty dynamics.

In the first Essay *A Growth-Poverty Paradox* Isabel Günther empirically illustrates the biases in estimated national poverty dynamics if measurement errors induced by changing survey design are not appropriately taken into account.

It is shown that previous poverty assessments of Burkina Faso neglected some important data inconsistencies over time, which led to the so-called Burkinabè Growth-Poverty-Paradox in the 1990s, with estimated increasing poverty rates despite sustained macro-economic growth. The revised estimates by the author, which account for changing survey design, indicate that poverty indeed decreased in the 1990s, i.e. growth did, in contrast to what previous estimates suggested, significantly reduce poverty.

Whereas in the first Essay the author treats data limitations on consumption data of households, the Essay *Pro-Poor Growth and Inflation Inequality* treats data limitations on (consumption) prices of households. In the last years several authors have proposed numerous definitions to measure pro-poor growth, i.e. to what extent the poor benefit from economic growth. However, all those measures have ignored varying inflation rates of households across the income distribution. The author rightly argues that incorporating varying inflation rates across the income distribution into measures of pro-poor growth is critically important, as one is interested in the real (and not nominal) change of the income of the poor - in relation to the non-poor. Moreover, for the case of Burkina Faso, it is illustrated that ignoring inflation inequality can severely bias empirical assessments of pro-poor growth.

In the Essay *Vulnerability to Idiosyncratic and Covariate Shocks*, Isabel Günther proposes a simple method to empirically assess the impact of idiosyncratic and covariate shocks on households' poverty risk. The proposed method can be used in a wide context, as it relies on commonly available cross-sectional household surveys and not on panel data, which most alternative methods to estimate vulnerability require. It is shown that the previous focus on available panel data of rural areas as well as on selected shocks might have both neglected existing poverty risk in urban areas as well as underestimated the impact of idiosyncratic shocks on households' consumption. For the case of Madagascar the estimation reveals that idiosyncratic shocks have an absolute higher impact on both rural and urban consumption than covariate shocks, but that covariate shocks have a comparatively higher impact on rural consumption.

Whereas shocks cause severe consumption fluctuations over time, employment changes have been identified as the most important factor for a sustained move in or out of poverty. Thus, in the Essay *A Competitive and Segmented La-*

*bor Market* the informal sector - the labor market of the poor - is analyzed in more detail. One question that arises from a dynamic welfare perspective is whether the poor are poor because they are trapped in the informal sector (market segmentation), or if they choose to work in the informal sector because they actually maximize their earnings in this sector (competitive markets). Previous studies have largely be constrained by missing panel data, that would allow to track employment changes of individuals over time. Hence, in this last Essay Isabel Günther formulates an econometric model, which allows to study the dynamics of the informal sector without comprehensive survey data. For the case of the urban labor market in Côte d'Ivoire it is shown that the informal sector is composed both of a segment where employment is the result of market segmentation and another part being the result of competitive labor markets.

The proposed methods and applications in the four essays constitute an important step forward in seeking more accurate estimates of both macro and micro poverty estimates over time. Certainly, more comprehensive panel data sets to measure poverty over time would be ideal. However, as the author rightly argues, the current question for research and policy is whether the time dimension of poverty should be ignored until the data requirements for the analysis of poverty dynamics are met; or if it might instead be useful to think about alternative methods for the empirical analysis of poverty dynamics - using currently available data sets - until the dimension of time is appropriately incorporated into household surveys. With the essays in this volume Isabel Günther contributes significantly to this latter research and greatly enhances the current economic literature on the empirical analysis of poverty dynamics.

Göttingen, June 2007
Prof. Stephan Klasen, Ph.D.

# Thanks for...

*Science is organized knowledge. Wisdom is organized life.*
Immanuel Kant, 1724-1804

**...the Science.** The person without whom I would not even have *started* this thesis is Stephan Klasen. Therefore, I'd like to thank him most for taking the risk of supervising an 'outsider' to the field of development economics. His enthusiasm for this science led me to 'organize' as much knowledge about development economics as possible in the last three years and the wish to keep on going. Also many thanks to him for giving me at the same time all the freedom *and* all the guidance I needed (and at the end of the thesis: all the pressure I needed). Most important: many thanks for all the fun working at the chair.

Next, I would like to thank my co-authors Michael Grimm, Ken Harttgen, and Andrey Launov without whom I would not have *finished* this thesis (at least not within 3 years). Michael taught me how to write a paper, Ken how to finish a paper and Andrey how to review a paper (if necessary a 100 times). Besides, I learned from them the *beauty* of STATA (Michael), LATEX (Ken) and ECONOMETRICS (Andrey). All of them shared with me their talent to be organized and patient, characteristics that are essential to finish a thesis and at the same time definitely not a particular strengths of mine. I am deeply grateful for their support, and especially for Andrey's last-minute help.

Last, I would like to mention all my other colleagues without whom I would not have *kept up* writing this thesis. Thanks to all for the really nice working atmosphere, but especially to my friend Melanie Grosse. A day without a coffee break and chat at her office is only half a day and a thesis without her corrections is a spelling mess. Not to forget to mention Ruben and Ruben who taught me everything I wanted (and I didn't want to know) about Bayern München and

Werder Bremen. Also thanks to Eva Söbbecke and Yvonne Treichel for always being in a good mood at the end of the corridor; and to the 'Göttinger' Bakary Kinde in Ouagadougou for making me feel at home in Western Africa; and last, to Elke Büsing, Alex Freese, Knut Gummert, Nils Klann, and Simon Lange, because they asked me to (and because it was a lot of fun working with them).

**...the Wisdom.** Thanks to all my 'old' friends, who kept being my friends in the last three years. Particular, to my two best friends, Miriam Laure for always listening to my thoughts and Florian Holz for taking care of my (not always very thoughtful) actions and for even 'supervising' me in Western Africa. I am also grateful for two 'new' friends, who made me stay in Göttingen: Claas Michaelis and Matthias Henze. I did not really fall in love with Göttingen and thought more than twice of moving. However, Claas did everything to make me love Göttingen (or at least accept it) and Matthias provided me with a refugee camp in Hamburg whenever Claas did not succeed.

I'd also very much like to thank my roommates (altogether 9), who 'supervised' my private life in Göttingen: Especially Tobias Hessler for his gorgeous smile every morning, Anita Schroven for hours of good afternoon tea, Thomas Maloney for our regular 'late-night' talks and Claudia Lein for always having a lot of fun with her. And last but not least, I am very grateful for my parents' wisdom and love in the last three years and for always supporting whatever I was doing (even if there was no reason behind it).

**...the Science and Wisdom.** My last and deepest thanks go to Ken. In the last three years, I have not only shared my office with him, but also every thought, emotion and chewing gum I had between Monday and Friday. I spent 7 hours a day, 5 days a week with him and I enjoyed every minute of it. I further thank him for not only accepting but also organizing both my chaotic work and life in the last three years. Although being happy to finish this thesis, I will definitely miss *the office*.

Göttingen, January 2007
Isabel Günther

# Contents

# List of Tables

# List of Figures

# List of Abbreviations

| | |
|---|---|
| AFD | Agence Française de Développement |
| CFA-Franc | Franc de la Communauté Financière d'Afrique |
| Coeff. | Coefficient |
| COL | Cost-Of-Living |
| CPI | Consumer Price Index |
| DHS | Demographic and Health Surveys |
| EP | Enquêtes Prioritaires |
| FGLS | Feasible Generalized Least Squares |
| FGT | Foster-Greer-Thorbecke Poverty Measure |
| GDP | Gross Domestic Product |
| GNI | Gross National Income |
| GIC | Growth Incidence Curve |
| HDI | Human Development Index |
| HH | Household |
| HIPC | Highly Indebted Poor Country |
| IAP | Instrument Automatisé de Prévision |
| ILO | International Labor Organization |
| INSD | Institut National de la Statistique et de la Démographie |
| IMF | International Monetary Fund |
| LSMS | Living Standard Measurement Survey |
| MDG | Millennium Development Goal |
| ML | Maximum Likelihood |

| | |
|---|---|
| NA | National Accounts |
| Obs. | Observation |
| OLS | Ordinary Least Squares |
| OPPG | Operationalizing Pro-Poor Growth |
| P0 | Poverty Headcount |
| P1 | Poverty Gap or Poverty Depth |
| P2 | Poverty Severity |
| pc | per capita |
| PCPI | Percentile Specific Consumer Price Index |
| PL | Poverty Line |
| PPG | Pro-Poor Growth |
| PPP | Purchasing Power Parity |
| PRSP | Poverty Reduction Strategy Paper |
| SAP | Structural Adjustment Program |
| SSA | Sub-Saharan Africa |
| Std. | Standard |
| UNDP | United Nations Development Program |

# Introduction and Overview

*Believe those who are seeking the truth. Doubt those who find it.*
Andre Gide, 1869 - 1951

## The Concept and Measurement of Poverty

Not many development economists would contradict the statement that understanding and reducing poverty lies at the heart of development economics and also public attention on the 'end of poverty' (Sachs, 2005) has sharply increased within the last decade. The question is however, *which* poverty to understand, reduce and end? But despite 50 years of intensive research as well as political debate, the concept of poverty is still evolving with an ever increasing number of definitions and measures of poverty. Although all definitions contain the notion of individuals living in some 'intolerable conditions', the question of relevant conditions and the ambiguity of the term intolerable led to quite different concepts.

It might be argued, that an emphasis on poverty definitions is anyhow misplaced and research should rather concentrate on the causes of poverty. However, different definitions of poverty might not only change our assessment of worldwide poverty but also our strategies to 'end' poverty. Hence, a fuzzy concept of poverty is not helpful and one should be clear, *which* poverty is to be analyzed and reduced.

There will never evolve any 'best' or 'right' poverty measure which can be agreed on, because poverty is in the end a normative issue and different concepts will always measure different aspects of poverty rather than provide a comprehensive 'right' assessment of poverty. The debate on poverty concepts and measurement should hence be seen as a framework to think about the different aspects of poverty rather than seeking for an ultimate measure of poverty. This framework on poverty thinking can, in principle, be summarized along four major lines, which are briefly discussed - without having the objective to be comprehensive - in the following:

## Poverty Dimensions

The first issue concerns the question of an appropriate measure for the living standards of the poor. Is a *money-metric* indicator, such as income, an appropriate and sufficient measure or do we have to consider (several) additional dimensions of *human* wellbeing.

Building on Amartya Sen's theoretical work (1985; 1999) on 'capabilities and functionings',[1] proponents of multidimensional poverty concepts argue that income is but one of many means to increase human wellbeing. Income should hence be seen as an input to an individual's standard of living rather than a direct measure of it, which should rather be conceptualized and measured with direct wellbeing outcomes, such as being safe, healthy, educated, well-sheltered, employed, etc. (see e.g. Klasen, 2000).

Today, there seems to be a wide consensus both among researchers and politicians that poverty is a multidimensional phenomenon, and, that poverty can only insufficiently be approximated by money-metric measures, even if income and other dimensions of wellbeing are often highly correlated (Kanbur and Squire, 2001). This is most prominently reflected in international measures of poverty, e.g. in the Human Development Index (HDI)[2] as well as in the Millennium Development Goals (MDGs)[3] - both analyzing multidimensional poverty -, but also in comprehensive survey data on the various dimensions of poverty, either col-

[1]Amartya Sen emphasizes that income is only valuable in so far it increases the 'capabilities' of individuals and thereby permitted 'functionings' in society.

[2]The Human Development Index (HDI) has the objective to measure people's wellbeing going beyond an income indicator. It is a weighted composite indicator of GDP per capita, life expectancy, school enrollment and literacy rates (UNDP, 2005). It was developed by the United Nations Development Program (UNDP) in 1990 and applied worldwide every year since then.

[3]In 2000 the world's nations as well as all major development institutions agreed on eight Millennium Devolopment Goals - which comprise various dimensions of people's wellbeing - to be achieved by 2015 (United Nations, 2005).

lected in general living standard measurement surveys (LSMS) or in specifically designed demographic and health surveys (DHS).

## Poverty Perspectives

The second question deals with the perspective to be taken when assessing the wellbeing of individuals. This refers on the one hand to the question, whether poverty should be defined as *absolute* or *relative* deprivation, and on the other hand to the question, whether an *objective* or *subjective* perspective is appropriate.

Although often Townsend (1971) is cited for first discussing relative deprivation, poverty has indeed been analyzed both from an absolute and a relative perspective since the very early economic literature. Already Smith (1776) described the 'necessaries' of life as a relative deprivation of society and not only as a failure to meet a minimum subsistence level.[4]

Today, the international community often takes an absolute perspective for developing countries - where poverty lines are based on a minimum calorie intake - and a relative perspective for developed countries - where poverty lines are defined as a percentage of the mean or median income of a given population. For example, the World Bank currently applies a one US$ PPP per capita per day poverty line to developing countries whereas the European Union defines the poor as people with an income below a poverty line of 60 percent of the median income in the country in which they live.[5]

In contrast, the discussion and measurement of subjective poverty versus 'objective' measures of poverty is rather new. From a subjective perspective, anyone can be absolutely and/or relatively poor, depending on the individual's own interpretation of his or her situation. This debate does not only refer to a subjective

[4]'By necessaries I understand not only the commodities which are indispensably necessary for the support of life, but what ever the customs of the country renders it indecent ... to be without. A linen shirt, for example, is, strictly speaking, not a necessary of life ... But in the present times, through the greater part of Europe, a creditable day-laborer would be ashamed to appear in public without a linen shirt ... Custom, in the same manner, has rendered leather shoes a necessary of life in England' (Smith, 1776).

[5]In 1985 the European Commission stated that those 'persons whose resources are so limited as to exclude them from the minimum acceptable way of life in the member state in which they live' (ECC, 1985) are considered to be poor.

'cut-off' below which an individual is considered to be poor, but also to a subjective relevant indicator of wellbeing to be analyzed. Note that this strand of research has mostly been applied in a national rather than in an individual context, i.e. not individual-specific but rather cultural-specific subjective poverty definitions have been revealed. As the understanding of poverty might widely differ across nations - it is argued - subjective wellbeing should be more relevant than a predefined objective but 'arbitrary' indicator and 'cut-off line' for poverty.

Recently, their is an increasing number of qualitative studies which try to reveal subjective understandings of poverty. Most well-known here is probably the research around the World Value Survey (WVS) or the 'Voices of the Poor' study by Narayan et al. (2000). Moreover, a 'subjective' question to derive an 'objective' national poverty line subjectively is now often included in standard living standard measurement surveys (LSMS).[6]

## Poverty Severity

Besides the identification of a relevant welfare indicator (the poverty dimension) and cut-off below which we consider individuals as poor (the poverty perspective), we should also be concerned with the scale of poverty (the poverty severity). The easiest measure of the magnitude of poverty - and also by far the most often applied in empirical analysis - is the poverty headcount, simply counting the number of people which fall below a certain cut-off (poverty line) in a certain poverty dimension.

Obviously such an index is a very rough indicator of the severity of poverty and has several undesirable axiomatic properties (for a discussion see e.g. Sen, 1976). Since the very early literature on the measurement of poverty several measures have therefore been developed, which also take into account the severity of poverty. This means they go beyond a dichotomous measure of poverty, simply dividing the population into the poor and non-poor, making a difference between the magnitude of poverty among the poor (e.g. Foster et al., 1984; Sen, 1976; Watts, 1968). Despite these long-standing advances, the poverty headcount is still

[6]Basically, the question is: 'How much income would you need to consider yourself as well-off?'

widely used; probably because it has - in contrast to many other measures - a quite intuitive interpretation and is therefore more attractive to policy makers.

The previous three classifications of poverty measures have long been discussed, mostly separately but also the 'whole' framework has been covered. For example Sen (1976; 1983; 1992) refers to poverty dimensions, perspectives, and severity as poverty space, identification, and aggregation. In contrast, the last aspect of poverty, which will be discussed in the following, namely 'time', has until recently somewhat been neglected in the discourse on the definition of poverty.

## Poverty Dynamics

Time in poverty analysis can refer to both static *snap-shot* versus *dynamic* poverty measures as well as to *ex-post* (or actual) versus *ex-ante* (or potential) poverty analysis. There is a long history of thinking about poverty over time on the macro-level both from a theoretical perspective, i.e. why some nations might be trapped into poverty while others escape (e.g. Smith, 1776), as well as from an empirical perspective, i.e. measuring changes in national or international wellbeing over time (see e.g. the World Development Report).

To the contrary, the study of micro-level poverty dynamics, i.e. individuals moving in and out of poverty, i.e. the study of chronic versus transient poverty, had been largely neglected until the 1990s - also due to data limitations, more precisely because of a lack of panel data. However, time or duration certainly is an important dimension for the understanding of individuals' current as well as lifetime well-being (Baulch and Hoddinott, 2000). In addition, 'time' allows for a distinction between structural and stochastic poverty as well as for an incorporation of the notion of risk in wellbeing analysis. This should certainly be of relevance if we assume that individuals are risk-averse.

Moreover, the concept of poverty dynamics has moved from an ex-post to an ex-ante analysis of poverty dynamics, acknowledging that individuals' current (or past) wellbeing might not be a good indicator of their poverty risk - or in other words their vulnerability to poverty (Calvo and Dercon, 2005) - which might not only have an impact on individuals' future but also on their current wellbeing. This literature is, however, still in its infancy both from a conceptual as well as from a methodological perspective.

Last, closely related to poverty dynamics is an analysis of the causes of poverty: With static measures, i.e. without a time dimensions, one cannot go beyond an analysis of the correlates of poverty. Analysis of poverty dynamics - both from a macro- as well as from a micro-perspective - is hence important to understand the causes of poverty, and not only the correlates of poverty, which has so far dominated the empirical literature.

## The Empirical Analysis of Poverty Dynamics

The scientific discourse on poverty measurement has (or at least should have) the objective to analyze 'real-world' poverty, as poverty reduction does not only lie at the heart of development economics but also at the 'heart' of many people both in developing as well as in developed countries. Hence, and as already briefly discussed, the conceptual debate on poverty is carried over to empirical analysis.

The empirical analysis of poverty has greatly been simplified in the last decade by a tremendous increase of available micro-level data[7] as well as by a rapid technological progress in information technologies to store and analyze these data sets (Bardhan, 2005). However, the empirical application of several poverty concepts - and this is until now especially true for the analysis of poverty dynamics, which is a rather recent studied dimension of poverty - is still constrained by data limitations as well as by an overall lack of data.

In the analysis of poverty dynamics, limited data has often been assumed away, which might have led to biased assessments of poverty dynamics in the past (see Essay 1 and Essay 2). Moreover, missing data has often led to data driven concepts, rather than to new surveys being based on relevant poverty concepts. This has - at least in the past - led to a neglect of certain aspects of poverty dynamics (see Essay 3 and Essay 4).

Thus the four essays in this thesis deal with different aspects of the *Empirical Analysis of Poverty Dynamics*, explicitly taking into account present data limitations. Certainly, more comprehensive data to measure poverty over time would be ideal. The question is, if the 'time' dimension of poverty should be ignored until the data requirements for the analysis of poverty dynamics are met. Or, if

[7] For example the living standard measurement surveys (LSMS) of the World Bank which are now available for most developing countries.

it might be useful to think about alternative methods for the empirical analysis of poverty dynamics - using currently available data sets - until the dimension of time is appropriately - also with the help of such work - incorporated into micro-level surveys.

## Macro Poverty Dynamics and Limited Data

Essay 1 and Essay 2, which are both based on joint work with Michael Grimm, discuss difficulties related to limited data in the analysis of aggregate poverty dynamics.[8] Even if there has been a long interest in national poverty dynamics, many surveys are still designed to give the most 'appropriate' static picture of poverty rather than 'accurate' estimates of national poverty dynamics. Or in other words, even if only (several) cross-sectional surveys are needed to analyze aggregate poverty dynamics, these cross-sectional data sets still have to be comparable over time, which is often not the case.

It has been argued that many estimates of poverty dynamics are biased by measurement errors induced by changing survey design or data collection, which might considerably reduce a clear monitoring of poverty over time. Moreover, with the increase of conditional development aid, some 'measurement error' might also be induced by political considerations to 'negotiate' numbers, i.e. to change methodologies over time, following Orwell's (1949) Ministry of Truth: 'who controls the past (figures), controls the future (aid flow)'.[9]

But although the problems - at least related to data collection and methodology - have theoretically widely been discussed (Deaton, 1997), they are often ignored in the empirical analysis of poverty dynamics. Moreover, poverty estimates, once published, are often assumed to reflect 'true' poverty changes, without questioning the underlying data or method anymore. Thus survey and data inconsistencies might often be responsible for a large part of 'unexplained' or 'surprising' poverty in- or decreases of countries, which otherwise show the same macro-economic performance.

Essay 1 empirically illustrates the biases in estimated poverty dynamics if 'survey dynamics', i.e. changing methods in collecting and/or processing data, are

[8]Here, aggregate poverty dynamics refer to poverty dynamics on the national level.

[9]Ali Achour, Economist *Coopération Française*, Ouagadougou.

not appropriately taken into account for the case of Burkina Faso. It is shown that previous poverty assessments of Burkina Faso neglected some important survey and data inconsistencies, which led to the so-called 'Burkinabè Growth-Poverty-Paradox' in the 1990s, with estimated increasing poverty rates despite sustained macro-economic growth and stagnant inequality. Revised estimates, which account for 'survey dynamics', indicate that poverty indeed decreased between 1994 and 2003, i.e. growth did, in contrast to what previous poverty estimates suggested, significantly reduce poverty.

Whereas Essay 1 treats data limitations on income or consumption of households, Essay 2 treats data limitations on (consumption) prices of households. Whenever income is compared across space or time, real and not nominal income is of interest. Or in other words, poverty is not only determined by a lack of income but also by a lack of purchasing power, which is a function of income and prices (see also Sen, 1981). Differences in purchasing power are widely acknowledged in welfare comparisons *across* developing countries (e.g. Reddy and Pogge, 2005). Surprisingly, this debate has not really been carried over to compare changes in the purchasing power across time *within* developing countries.

Within the last decade there has been an intensive debate on whether growth accrues as much to the poor as to the non-poor. For this analysis various measures of pro-poor growth (PPG) have been defined, which have however - at least in their empirical application - ignored (different) changes in the purchasing power of households across the income distribution.

In Essay 2 it is first of all argued, that considering varying inflation rates across the income distribution is a theoretical necessity in the measurement of pro-poor growth. Moreover, for the case of Burkina Faso, it is illustrated that ignoring inflation inequality in PPG measures can severely bias empirical assessments of pro-poor growth. Hence, in Essay 2 simple methods are suggested to redress such biases, for the growth incidence curve (Ravallion and Chen, 2003) and the decomposition of poverty changes (Datt and Ravallion, 1992) as two PPG measures.

## Micro Poverty Dynamics and Missing Data

Essay 3 and Essay 4 discuss difficulties related to missing data in the analysis of micro-level poverty dynamics. Hence, data in these two essays is not only limited - as in Essay 1 and Essay 2 - but even completely missing. Moreover, whereas Essay 1 and Essay 2 have dealt with the *ex-post measurement of poverty dynamics on the macro-level*, Essay 3 and Essay 4 address the *ex-ante analysis of poverty dynamics on the micro-level*. Last, Essay 3 and Essay 4 also incorporate an analysis of the causes of poverty dynamics rather than a pure measurement of it. As argued, measurement of poverty is important but does not always help to understand why it occurs, which is important to know for policy interventions to address the causes and not only the symptoms of poverty.

Whereas comparison of poverty over time has long been undertaken on a national level it is only since recently that poverty dynamics on a household level are studied. The problem being that the former can also be analyzed with cross-sectional data whereas the latter would ideally require panel data, which is still missing for most developing countries. Hence, empirical analysis of poverty risk, or vulnerability to poverty, is still rare.

In Essay 3, which is based on joint work with Kenneth Harttgen, a simple method is proposed to empirically assess the impact of idiosyncratic and covariate shocks on households' vulnerability to poverty. The proposed method can be used in a wide context, as it relies on commonly available cross-section living standard measurement surveys (LSMS). It is an integration of multilevel modeling into Chaudhuri's (2002) approach to estimate ex-ante the mean and variance of households' consumption with cross-sectional data.

It is shown, that the previous focus on available panel data of rural areas as well as on selected shocks might have both neglected existing poverty risk in urban areas as well as underestimated the impact of idiosyncratic shocks on households' consumption. For the case of Madagascar we estimate that idiosyncratic shocks have a higher impact on both rural and urban consumption than covariate shocks. However, whereas covariate shocks have a comparatively higher impact on rural consumption, idiosyncratic shocks have a comparatively higher impact on urban households' vulnerability.

Whereas shocks cause severe wellbeing fluctuations over time, employment changes have been identified as the most important factor for a *sustained* move in or out of poverty (e.g. Fields et al. 2003; Woolard and Klasen, 2005).[10] Hence,

[10]Moreover, also aggregated national poverty reduction is largely determined by the extent to which macro economic growth translates into employment opportunities (for the poor). See var-

in Essay 4 the informal sector, which is said to be the labor market of the poor in developing countries, is analyzed in more detail.

One question that arises from a dynamic welfare perspective is, whether the poor are trapped into the informal sector and thus into poor earnings opportunities (market segmentation). Or, if they choose to work in the informal sector, because given their characteristics, this is actually where they can maximize their earnings (competitive markets). In other words, are individuals poor because they are employed in the informal sector or are they employed in the informal sector because they are poor(ly endowed). This question can in general only be answered from a dynamic perspective, which either requires panel or retrospective data.

However, both panel data, that would allow to track employment changes of individuals over time, as well as retrospective information on the causes of (poor) people moving into the informal sector, is missing for most developing countries. In Essay 4, which is based on joint work with Andrey Launov, an econometric model is formulated, which allows to study the dynamics of the informal sector without panel data and without information on the reasons of people working in the informal sector. The proposed method is an integration of Heckmann selection bias (1979) into finite mixture models. For the case of the urban labor market in Côte d'Ivoire it is shown that the informal sector is in fact composed of two unobserved segments, with part of informal employment being the result of labor market segmentation and the other part being the result of competitive labor markets.

## Poverty Dynamics in Africa

As already indicated, the proposed methods for the analysis of poverty dynamics are applied to household survey data from various sub-Saharan Africa (SSA) countries; namely to Burkina Faso, with a headcount poverty rate of 46.3 percent and a HDI rank of 174,[11] to Côte d'Ivoire, with a poverty rate of 44.0 and a HDI rank of 164, and to Madagascar, with a poverty rate of 72.1 and a HDI rank of 143 (World Bank, 2005). Here, not only the empirical implementation of

ious studies of the 'Operationalizing Pro-Poor Growth' (OPPG) Research Program of the World Bank.

[11] 177 countries are ranked according to their HDI in the Human Development Report.

the discussed methodologies but also the consequences for our understanding of poverty dynamics are illustrated, which should be especially relevant for African countries.

It seems to be a stylized fact (see e.g. Sachs, 2005) that in the last decade poverty reduction in sub-Saharan Africa has been the slowest from a cross-country perspective or even non-existent - by almost all of the currently used concepts or definitions of poverty. An accurate measurement and understanding of the underlying poverty dynamics both on the macro as well as on the micro level, therefore, seems to be most important for these countries to eventually increase poverty reduction in the future. Moreover, especially in these poorest SSA countries is micro-economic data often very limited or even missing.

The proposed methodologies can certainly not perfectly reflect 'true' poverty dynamics neither on the macro- nor on the micro-level. However, they should constitute a step forward in 'seeking true' estimates of poverty dynamics. In addition, they can also contribute to the discussion on how the 'time dimension' of poverty can be integrated into standard household surveys. Last - although being empirical - the methodological discussions as well as the empirical results of the four essays should also be used as a starting point for a reflection on the current underlying theories of poverty dynamics.

# Essay 1

# A Growth-Poverty-Paradox?

*There are no facts, only interpretations.*
Friedrich Nietzsche, 1844-1900

**Abstract:** It is a stylized fact, that some countries do not show significant poverty reduction despite considerable growth rates, whereas others succeed in reducing poverty with only moderate or even negative growth rates. In this paper we ask the question whether part of this missing link between growth and poverty can be explained by sole survey and data inconsistencies, with an empirical illustration for Burkina Faso. We show that previous poverty assessments of Burkina Faso neglected some important survey and data issues which led to the so-called 'Burkinabè Growth-Poverty-Paradox' in the 1990s, with increasing poverty rates despite sustained macro-economic growth and stagnant inequality. Our revised estimates indicate that poverty significantly decreased between 1994 and 2003, i.e. growth did - in contrast to what previous poverty estimates suggested - significantly reduce poverty.

---

based on joint work with Michael Grimm.

## 1.1 Introduction

In the last decade, an extensive literature on the empirical relationship between growth and poverty, i.e. the impact of macro-economic growth on micro-economic poverty reduction has emerged (e.g. Dollar and Kray, 2002; Ravallion, 2001; Ravallion and Chen, 1997). One stylized fact of this empirical literature seems to be that *on average* 'growth is good for the poor' (Dollar and Kray, 2002) with growth *on average* leading to considerable poverty reduction, with an *average* estimated growth elasticity of poverty of -2 (for an overview see Ram, 2006), but with country specific elasticities lying anywhere between about -5 and 5 (Figure 1.1).

Figure 1.1: Growth-Elasticity of Poverty in the 1990's

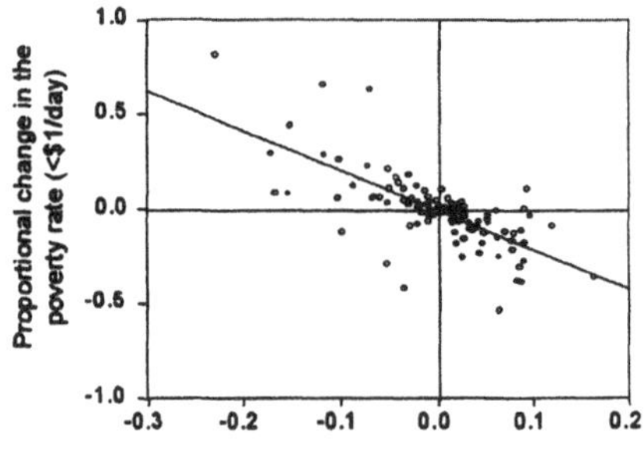


*Source:* Ravallion, 2001.

In response to the observed cross-country heterogeneity in growth elasticities of poverty, several studies have tried to explain the diverse impact of growth on poverty reduction. This literature can broadly be divided into theoretically motivated and policy-motivated studies.

The former argues that a large part of the differences in growth elasticities of poverty across countries can already be explained theoretically by an 'identity' linking growth to poverty reduction (Bourguignon, 2003; Klasen and Misselhorn, 2006). More precisely, the growth elasticity of poverty of a given country is a function of (i) the initial inequality, (ii) the initial development level,[1] and (iii) the change in inequality of a country (Bourguignon, 2003).

The latter, mainly policy-motivated literature, tries to identify the main national as well as international policies that have increased (or decreased) the impact of growth on poverty reduction in the last decade (see e.g. Dorwad et al., 2004; Kray, 2003; Lopez, 2003; Ravallion and Datt, 1999 or the 'Operationalizing Pro-Poor Growth' (OPPG) Research Program of the World Bank).

In this paper we make a third attempt to explain the diverse experience of countries, namely attributing part of the observed heterogeneity of growth elasticities of poverty to significant survey and data inconsistencies over time that exist not only between countries but also within countries. One interesting case in point here is Burkina Faso.

Burkina Faso is still one of the poorest countries in the world, with a Gross Domestic Product (GDP) per capita of 384 US$ PPP (IMF, 2005) and a Human Development Index (HDI) rank of 174 out of 177 countries (UNDP, 2005). However, according to National Accounts (NA) data, Burkina Faso has experienced relatively strong economic growth over the last decade. After the devaluation of the *Franc de la Communauté Financière d'Afrique* (CFA-Franc) in January 1994, real GDP per capita began to rise, with an average of 2 percent growth per year.[2]

According to the International Monetary Fund (IMF) this good economic performance is, first of all, the result of the gains in competitiveness following the devaluation of the CFA-Franc, the large public investment program (mainly externally financed), and the financial and structural policies (including price and trade liberalization) within the framework of structural adjustment programs (SAP), aimed at consolidating the market orientation of the economy and maintaining macro-economic stability (IMF, 2003).

Despite the considerable macro-economic growth in the last years the micro-economic performance has so far been rather disappointing. Official poverty estimates, including those of the Burkinabè Statistical Office, the World Bank, and the

[1] Here, the development level of a country is defined as the location of the poverty line relative to mean income.

[2] Source: *Instrument Automatisé de Prévision* (IAP). This is a macro-economic framework based on NA data developed by the Burkinabè Ministry of Economy and Development with technical assistance of the German *Gesellschaft für Technische Zusammenarbeit*. It is considered as the most reliable macro-economic data source in Burkina Faso.

United Nations Development Program (UNDP), all derived from 1994, 1998, and 2003 household survey data, indicated that the poverty headcount index stagnated at a high level of roughly 45 percent between 1994 and 2003, implying that the growth elasticity of poverty was zero (Fofack et al., 2001; INSD, 2003; Lachaud, 2003).

The simultaneous occurrence of strong positive growth and stagnating poverty rates suggests that inequality increased significantly during this period. However, according to the official estimates inequality remained constant with a Gini coefficient of 0.46. This led to the so-called 'Burkinabè Growth-Poverty-Paradox', with increasing poverty rates despite sustained macro-economic growth and constant inequality rates.

Several explanations might be given for this 'paradox'. First, macro-economic growth might have been completely disconnected from households' expenditures: the 'missing link' hypothesis. In other words increases in GDP per capita were mainly driven by enterprise benefits, investments, government consumption or by increases in consumption of rather few agents not necessarily covered by household surveys and/or went outside the country. Second, it is also possible that macro-economic growth was simply over-estimated. In many developing countries, and Burkina Faso is no exception, it is very hard to obtain reliable statistics on sector-specific value added and population growth.

However, between 1994 and 2003 not only GDP per capita, but also official estimates of private consumption per capita as measured in the National Accounts (NA) and as measured in the household surveys showed considerable (and quite similar) annual growth rates. Between 1994 and 2003 GDP per capita grew annually by 2.3 percent, private per capita consumption in the NA increased by 3.1 percent, and per capita consumption in the household surveys by 2.5 percent. Thus neither the 'missing link' hypothesis nor over-estimated macro-economic growth seems to be the cause for a zero growth elasticity of poverty between 1994 and 2003 in Burkina Faso.

Hence, a third point, concerning several methodological issues related to microeconomic survey design and poverty analysis, leading to time-inconsistent poverty estimates, might be largely responsible for the Growth-Poverty-Paradox.[3] The aim of this paper is, hence, to discuss and analyze these methodological problems in detail, to address them, and to offer a new growth, poverty, and inequality assessment for Burkina Faso. These new estimates do certainly not perfectly reflect the welfare changes that occurred in Burkina Faso between 1994 and 2003, but should constitute a considerable improvement to previous official poverty estimates.

We believe that most of the methodological problems discussed in this paper are not country-specific to Burkina Faso but should arise in other (least developed) countries as well. Hence, we think that this paper can also contribute to the current debate on the driving forces behind the heterogeneity of growth elasticities of poverty across countries. We therefore review some simple procedures to test and tackle the problem of inconsistent micro-economic data to estimate more reliable growth elasticities of poverty.

The paper is organized as follows. In Section 1.2, we shortly describe the recent economic development in Burkina Faso and explain in detail the 'Burkinabè Growth-Poverty-Paradox'. In Section 1.3, we analyze and address the 'paradox' by computing more time-consistent poverty and inequality estimates, which are presented in section 1.4. In Section 1.4, we furthermore undertake a robustness check of our new poverty and inequality estimates and present revised monetary (and non-monetary) growth elasticities of poverty. We conclude in Section 1.5.

## 1.2 The Paradox

Figure 1.2 shows the development of real GDP per capita between 1990 and 2003 in Burkina Faso. With the beginning of structural adjustment programs in 1991 real GDP per capita began to decline by approximately -3.8 percent per year until 1993. Then in 1994, the failure of the structural adjustment strategy in several countries of the CFA-Franc zone, and especially in one of the most important ones, Côte d'Ivoire, led to a 50 percent devaluation of the CFA-Franc parity in relation to the French Franc. After the devaluation - due to gains in competitiveness -

[3]Variations in the purchasing power of the poor relative to the non-poor in connection with an only weak integration of poor households into the macro-economic growth process solve the remaining part of the 'paradox'.

growth of real GDP per capita began to rise and averaged at approximately 3.3 percent per year between 1994 and 1998. This growth was further sustained by a favorable development of the world market price for cotton and an increase of the area used for cotton production.

Figure 1.2: Real GDP per capita

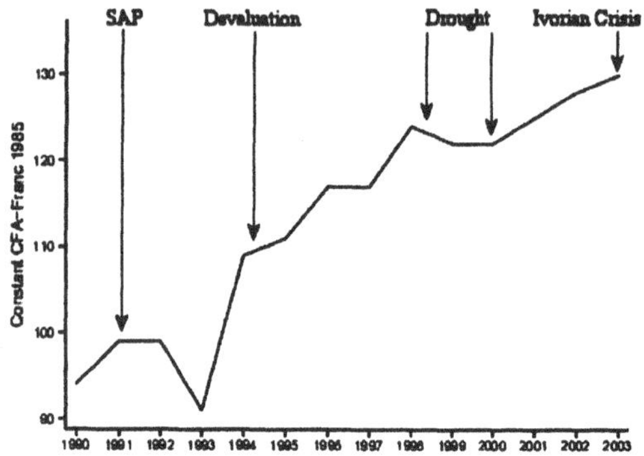


*Source:* IAP.

Real GDP per capita decreased in 1998 and stagnated in 2000 due to two consecutive years of drought but reached again a growth rate of around 2 percent in the following years. Since 2002 Burkina Faso has been affected by the Ivorian crisis (i.e. less trade with Côte d'Ivoire, higher transportation costs, immigration and lower private remittances), but growth in 2003 was still estimated at 6.8 percent. This was mainly due to a very good harvest in 2002/03 and a relatively fast reorganization of the country's import and export channels (AFD, 2003). Over the whole observation period 1994-2003, Burkina Faso pursued its efforts to undertake structural reforms, in particular price and trade liberalization. In May 2000, Burkina Faso established its first Poverty Reduction Strategy Paper (PRSP) and reached its completion point in the Heavily Indebted Poor Countries (HIPC) Initiative II in April 2002.

Given this overall good growth performance between 1994 and 2003, even if interrupted by two severe droughts, we would have expected a substantial decrease in poverty in Burkina Faso since 1990. Table 1.1 presents the official poverty and inequality estimates as presented in 2003 by the Burkinabè Statistics Office, by the *Institut National de la Statistique et de la Démographie* (INSD), by the UNDP and (for the period 1994 to 1998) also by the World Bank.[4] Poverty is measured as the headcount index of poverty, which is equivalent to $P0$ of the Foster-Greer-Thorbecke Poverty Measure $P\alpha$, where $\alpha$ is a parameter of inequality-aversion (Foster et al., 1984). In addition, Table 1.1 presents the official estimates for $P1$ - yielding the depth of poverty - and $P2$ - referring to the severity of poverty.[5]. Income (i.e. consumption) inequality is measured with the Gini Index, which can take any value between zero and one. Zero refers to 'perfect' equality with everyone having the same (mean) income within a country. One refers to 'perfect' inequality with all income within a country accruing to one person, and everyone else having zero income.

The figures in Table 1.1 indicate that, despite good macro-economic performance, poverty did not decrease but stagnated at a level of roughly 45 percent between 1994 and 2003. A simultaneous occurrence of economic growth and poverty stagnation would suggest that inequality increased during the observed period. But inequality was estimated with a Gini coefficient of around 0.46 over the whole period leading to the 'Burkinabè Growth-Poverty-Paradox'.

Table 1.1 also shows the official poverty line used for the computation of the poverty indices. The massive increase of the nominal poverty line between 1994 and 1998 and the still strong increase between 1998 and 2003 is striking. Whether this considerable nominal increase of the poverty line over time can be justified by the rise of the cost-of-living of the poor and how that relates to the development of the national Consumer Price Index (CPI) will be analyzed in detail in next section. We will show that the poverty line used in official estimates already explains a large part of the 'paradox'.

[4]The estimates are based on three national representative household surveys, the *Enquête Prioritaires* (EP), undertaken in 1994 (EPI), 1998 (EPII), and 2003 (EPIII). These surveys are similar to the World Bank's Living Standard Measurement Surveys (LSMS). In each survey round, the sample size was roughly 8,500 households and 60,000 individuals (without a panel dimension).

[5]$P0$, or the headcount index, measures the percentage of the population living below the poverty line. $P1$, or the poverty gap, is a measure of the average difference between income and the poverty line, with the difference for the non-poor set to zero. $P2$, or the severity of poverty, also takes into account the inequality among the poor.

Table 1.1: Poverty and Inequality Trends - Official Estimates

| | Urban | | | Rural | | | National | | |
|---|---|---|---|---|---|---|---|---|---|
| | 1994 | 1998 | 2003 | 1994 | 1998 | 2003 | 1994 | 1998 | 2003 |
| P0 | 10.4 | 16.5 | 19.9 | 51.0 | 51.0 | 52.3 | 44.5 | 45.3 | 46.4 |
| P1 | 2.5 | 4.0 | - | 16.1 | 15.7 | - | 13.9 | 13.7 | 15.6 |
| P2 | 0.9 | 1.5 | - | 7.0 | 6.8 | - | 6.0 | 5.9 | 7.1 |
| Gini | 0.45 | 0.51 | 0.49 | 0.38 | 0.37 | 0.39 | 0.46 | 0.46 | 0.46 |
| PL | | 1994 | | | 1998 | | | 2003 | |
| CFA F (Index 1994=100) | | 41,099(100.0) | | | 72,690(176.9) | | | 82,672(201.2) | |

*Source:* INSD (2003).
*Notes:* P0: poverty headcount. P1: poverty gap. P2: poverty severity. Gini: measure of inequality. No official estimates for P1 and P2 for urban and rural areas were provided in 2003. The national poverty line (PL) is expressed on a yearly per capita basis in current CFA prices. The Gini coefficient is population weighted.

# 1.3 Biased Poverty Estimates

In this section we argue that previous poverty assessments were seriously biased by three micro-economic methodological inconsistencies: an inconsistent poverty line over time, changes in the methodology used to compute household expenditure aggregates, and, to a lesser extent, changes in the household survey design (see Table 1.2 for an overview).

## 1.3.1 Poverty Line

Figure 1.3 shows that the official poverty line increased much more than the CPI between 1994 and 2003, implying that the 'prices of the poor' used for the computation of the poverty line increased more than the prices of goods consumed by the 'representative urban household' used for the computation of the CPI. More precisely, the national poverty line increased by 76.9 percent between 1994 and 1998 and by 13.7 percent between 1998 and 2003, whereas the national CPI increased by only 22.7 percent and 7.1 percent, respectively. Given that the location of the poverty line (over time) highly influences an assessment of poverty dynamics, we need to analyze whether this high inflation of the poverty line is indeed justified.

Figure 1.3: Cereal Prices & CPI & Official Poverty Line

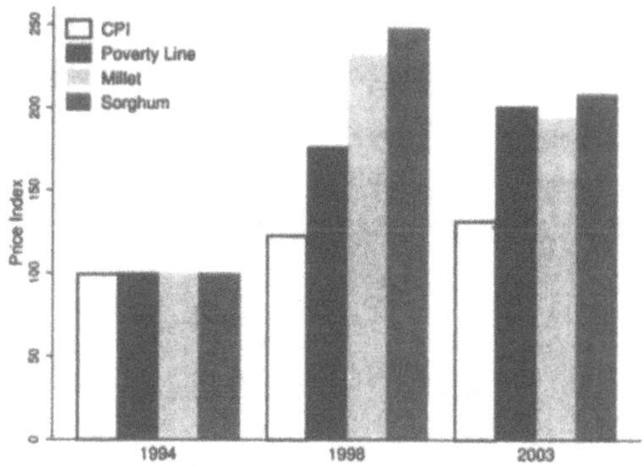


*Source:* CPI: IAP; Cereal Prices: Grain Market Price Surveillance System. Official Poverty Line: INSD (2003).
*Notes:* Prices are indexed to 1994=100. Cereal prices are annual averages.

There is no doubt that a poverty line should be composed of a higher 'basic' food component than the national CPI which usually reflects the consumption habits of an 'average' household[6] rather than the budget shares of the poor.[7] Indeed, Burkina Faso's official poverty lines in all three years (1994, 1998, and 2003) have a basic food component of more than 50 percent whereas the national CPI only has a food component of 10 percent. Hence, the poverty line cannot simply be inflated with the CPI if relative prices of basic food items changed over time.

In Burkina Faso, the CPI increased by only 22.7 percent between 1994 and 1998 whereas prices for cereals (for example millet and sorghum) more than doubled during the same period. Between 1998 and 2003 the CPI further increased while cereal food prices decreased (Figure 1.3). The inflationary surge of staple prices between 1994 and 1998 was mainly due to a severe drought in 1997/98 which reduced cereal production in this season by more than 20 percent with re-

[6]Note that an 'average' household is not the same as a 'representative' household, i.e. the CPI reflects the consumption habits of an 'average' household but is in general 'representative' for a rather rich household.

[7]See also Essay 2.

spect to 1996/97.[8] In addition, prices were driven by a general lack of productivity increase accompanied by high population growth.

Hence, the sharp inflation of the official poverty line between 1994 and 1998 is indeed justified given the massive price increase of cereals and given the consumption pattern of the poor. However, the further inflation of the poverty line between 1998 and 2003 cannot be justified by observed relative price changes, and was actually caused by a change of the underlying consumption basket (see also Table 1.2).

Table 1.2: Survey and Data Inconsistencies

| | Survey Year | | |
|---|---|---|---|
| | 1994 | 1998 | 2003 |
| Poverty Line | | | |
| Indexed Food Component | – | yes | yes |
| Indexed Non-Food Component | – | no | no |
| Non-Food/Food | 0.32 | 0.39 | 1.01 |
| Welfare Aggregate | | | |
| Rents Missing | 0.22 | 0.16 | 0.06 |
| Durables | not included | included | included |
| Adjustment to NA | no | yes | no |
| Survey Design | | | |
| Survey Period | Oct-Jan | May-Aug | Apr-Jul |
| Recall Period Food | 30 days | 15 days | 15 days |
| Consumption Items | 50 | 70 | 80 |

*Source:* EPI, EPII, EPIII.

More precisely, the official poverty line in 1994, 1998, and 2003 was based on the price of a 2,283 calorie food intake composed of millet, sorghum, maize, and rice, which are the main components of nutrition intake for poor people in Burkina Faso. Whereas this real food component was appropriately inflated with the respective price index over time, the non-food component was not inflated over time with the respective non-food price index, but was simply calculated as a share of the nominal food component, i.e. implicitly inflated with the food price index.

[8] Estimates are based on the agricultural survey, the *Enquête Permanente d'Agricole*, which is undertaken on a yearly basis in Burkina Faso.

Moreover, the ratio of the non-food to the food component was even altered over time. Whereas the non-food component was calculated, taking approximately 30-40 percent of the nominal non-food component in 1994 and 1998, in 2003 the non-food component was calculated taking 100 percent of the nominal food component.

This implies that both the inflation of the poverty line between 1994 and 1998 as well as between 1998 and 2003 was overestimated. Between 1994 and 1998 basic food prices increased much more than prices of other goods. Hence, implicitly inflating the non-food component with the food price index between 1994 and 1998 overestimates poverty in 1998 relative to 1994. Between 1998 and 2003 relative price changes between food and non-food items were less severe. However, now the massive increase of the non-food component (in relation to the nominal food component) induced again an upward bias of the nominal poverty line in 2003.

In other words, the price index implicit in the official poverty line does not correspond to a true Laspeyres (or Paasche) Index. Therefore, we suggest computing a new and more appropriate poverty line using constant real weights of food and non-food items over the period 1994 to 2003.

To compute such a time-consistent poverty line, we took the nominal value of the official poverty line in 2003, and the budget shares as they are observed in the household survey among households living below this line in 2003. The food crop component (consisting of maize, millet, sorghum, and rice) was then deflated to 1998 and to 1994 using the observed price changes for the corresponding cereals. The remaining food and non-food component was deflated with the CPI, with the price change of food crops netted out.[9]

We chose 2003 as the 'base' year for the poverty line and the estimated budget shares to be consistent with the latest official poverty estimates in Burkina Faso. Hence, in this application we preferred a Paasche Index to a Laspeyres Index mainly because of political reasons.[10] However, we also used the official poverty line and the budget shares among the poor of 1994 or 1998 as reference points

[9]We applied monthly-specific price indices. More precisely, we took the average prices of the respective four-months survey periods in 1994, 1998, and 2003.

[10]See also Essay 2.

to check the robustness of our results to a Laspeyres Index. We found the same poverty trends, only on a lower level.

There are several other methods to construct a national poverty 'baseline' to be in- or deflated over time. All of them involve some 'arbitrariness', but the probably most often used method for developing countries is based on a 'costs of basic needs' approach. First, the cost of a 2100-2300 calorie intake per capita,[11] which is widely considered as the minimum calorie intake of an individual (Deaton, 1997), is calculated. In general, this cost is defined as the food poverty or extreme poverty line. In a second step, the non-food component of the 'costs of basic needs' can be derived by calculating the food expenditure that households - whose total expenditure is equal to the food poverty line - are willing to give up for non-food consumption. This share of non-food consumption is added to the food poverty line to calculate the national poverty line. An alternative is to define the poverty line as the total expenditure of households that spend exactly the amount calculated in step one on food items.

We did not intend to derive a new more 'precise' poverty line, but rather to appropriately in- or deflate poverty lines over time, or in other words we were more interested in the budget shares of the poverty line than in the poverty line itself. Hence, to be consistent with the latest poverty line constructed by the Burkinabè Statistical Office - the INSD - we used the official poverty line of 2003 and calculated the average budget shares of the people living below this line to be deflated with the appropriate price indices. Thus, we did not calculate budget shares to construct a poverty line but used the poverty line to construct budget shares. Our approach should lead to an estimated food share that lies somewhere between the food share of poverty lines that are constructed with one of the two above described methods of the 'cost of basic needs' approach.

The revised poverty lines, which are presented in Table 1.3, show a somewhat lower inflation rate between 1994 and 1998 and a much lower inflation rate between 1994 and 2003 than the official poverty line.

[11] The reference group is some cut-off of the lower-part of the expenditure distribution.

Table 1.3: Official and Revised Poverty Lines

| | 1994 | 1998 | 2003 |
|---|---|---|---|
| Official Poverty Line | 41,099 (100.0) | 72,690 (176.9) | 82,672 (201.2) |
| Revised Poverty Line | 43,219 (100.0) | 82,885 (155.7) | 82,672 (155.3) |

*Source:* Official PL: INSD (2003). Revised PL: Computations by the authors.
*Notes:* Both poverty lines are expressed on a yearly per capita basis in current CFA prices. The implicit price index of the poverty line is expressed in parenthesis (1994=100).

### 1.3.2 Welfare Aggregate

All previous studies on the development of poverty in Burkina Faso used the same household expenditure aggregate. This aggregate was provided by the INSD in addition to the raw data of the household surveys. However, this aggregate was based on some assumptions which differ from the assumptions usually made when constructing household expenditure aggregates for poverty analysis. In addition, some of the necessary assumptions were not maintained in a consistent way over time. These biases and inconsistencies were recently also recognized by the World Bank and discussed in their 2004 poverty assessment (World Bank, 2004). It should however be emphasized that the INSD first of all tried to provide current 'snap-shot' poverty estimates and less a comparison over time, explaining why some inconsistent assumptions might have been made.

First, usually hypothetical rents for those households which own their housing are imputed (Deaton and Zaidi, 2002). Not doing so would underestimate the wellbeing of these households relative to those households who rent their housing. In Burkina Faso, roughly 90 percent of all households do not pay any housing rent. However, the official expenditure aggregate contains imputed values only for some house owners and they are missing for 22, 16, and 6 percent of all households in 1994, 1998 and 2003 respectively. This implies that poverty was always overestimated, but less so from year to year. We corrected this bias by imputing rents for all households where rents were not declared or not yet imputed.[12]

[12]We applied average regional urban and rural rents as a hedonic regression on rents did not yield any applicable results.

Second, usually expenditures for durables such as televisions, radios, refrigerators, motorcycles, bicycles, cars, or investments into housing, land, and livestock are not included in a welfare aggregate which is constructed to measure consumption and poverty for a given period of time, e.g. a year. The argument is that the utility drawn from durables concerns not only the period under consideration but also subsequent periods (Deaton and Zaidi, 2002). Given the lack of information allowing to divide the utility over the relevant periods or to compute appropriate user costs, expenditures for durables are usually excluded in poverty analysis. However, these expenditures were included in 1998 and 2003 with their total purchasing price, but were not included in 1994 in the Burkinabè welfare aggregate. Although this does not severely bias poverty estimates, as most durables are purchased by rather rich households, it does increase inequality measures. To redress this bias, we excluded expenditures for durables from the expenditure aggregates in 1998 and 2003.

Third, in 1998 the official expenditure aggregate was uniformly increased for all households by 12.4 percent. The reason for this adjustment is not well documented, but it seems that this was done to obtain a household expenditure aggregate closer to the National Accounts expenditure aggregate. Such an uniform adjustment can only hardly be justified, even more if it is only undertaken for one particular survey year. This adjustment clearly led to a substantial underestimation of poverty in 1998. In our estimates we did not follow such an adjustment, neither for 1998 nor for any other year.

In addition to the above described corrections, we applied regional deflators provided by the INSD to account for regional differences in the cost-of-living. For reasons of comparison with other studies, we divided total household expenditure by household size to obtain per capita expenditure and did not use any equivalence scales, i.e. no adjustments were made for economies of scale and/or differences in need by age and sex (Deaton, 1994). Since household composition did not change significantly in Burkina Faso between 1994 and 2003, using per capita instead of adult equivalence estimates might introduce a significant bias in poverty *levels*, especially if compared across households with different household structure, but should not considerably affect estimates of aggregate poverty *changes*.

### 1.3.3 Survey Design

The INSD has continuously improved the design of the household surveys in Burkina Faso, which might however have lowered the comparability of poverty estimates over time. More precisely, the survey design of the EPI, the EPII, and the EPIII differ in three major points: First, whereas the EPI was undertaken in the post-harvest period (October to January), the EPII and the EPIII were undertaken in the pre-harvest period (May to August). Second, whereas the EPI had a recall period for food items of 30 days the EPII and the EPIII had a recall period for food items of only 15 days. Third, the disaggregation of expenditures was continuously increased from 1994 to 2003 from 50 items in 1994 to 70 items in 1998 and 80 items in 2003 (Table 1.2). Such changes in survey design can have a considerable impact on poverty and inequality estimates.

First, it is often argued that in developing countries real household consumption in the pre-harvest season is considerably lower than in the post-harvest season. For example Dercon and Krishan (2002), using panel data of 1,450 rural Ethiopian households, show that differences in real food consumption before and after the harvest amounted up to 10 percent for the poorest households. Since we can observe high seasonal price fluctuations for the case of Burkina Faso (see Figure 1.4), we can assume that households in Burkina Faso considerable reduce their real consumption during the pre-harvest season and increase their real consumption during the post-harvest season.

Whether this leads to an in- or decrease in nominal household consumption is unclear and depends on the induced price changes. Annual price changes are however also covered by the poverty lines in 1994, 1998, and 2003, which use the observed food and non-food prices of the respective survey period. Thus, whether a household lies below or above the poverty line only depends on changes in real consumption and not on changes in prices. Hence, the fact that EPI was conducted in the post-harvest season whereas EPII and EPIII was conducted in the pre-harvest season implies that poverty in 1994 has been underestimated relative to poverty in 1998 and 2003.

Second, empirical studies show that longer recall periods lead to considerably lower declared expenditures. For example, Scott and Amenuvegbe (1990) show that for frequently purchased items reported expenditures fell at an average of

Figure 1.4: Seasonal Price Variations

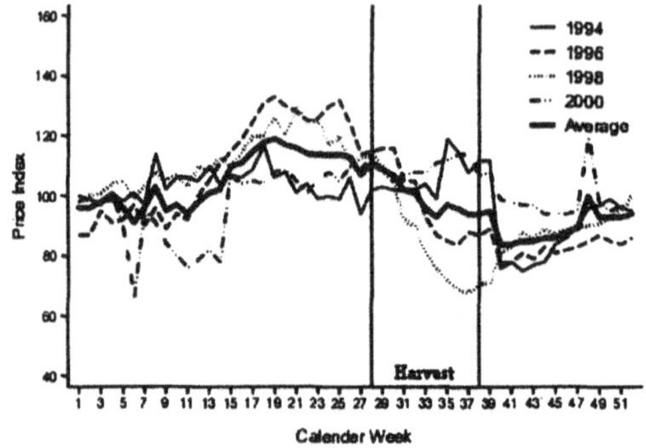


*Source:* Cereal prices: Grain Market Price Surveillance System.
*Notes:* In each year, prices are indexed to an average of 100.

2.9 percent for every day added in the Ghanaian LSMS. Deaton (2003a) reports an experiment with different recall periods in India where shortening the recall period for food items from 30 to 7 days resulted in a 30 percent higher food consumption. This implies that in Burkina Faso poverty in 1994, which had a recall period of 30 days for food expenditure (in contrast to 15 days for 1998 and 2003), was overestimated relative to poverty headcount estimates for 1998 and 2003.

Last, it has been shown, that a higher disaggregation of expenditure items leads to higher declared expenditures (Jolliffe, 2001; Lanjouw and Lanjouw, 2001). As the number of registered food and non-food items increased from 50 to 70 and to 80 items in 1994, 1998 and 2003, respectively, poverty in 1994 was underestimated relative to 1998 and 2003 and poverty in 1998 was still underestimated (although to a lesser extent) in comparison to 2003.

To achieve comparability of poverty estimates based on different household survey designs the literature suggests various methods, which, however, require rather strong assumptions and/or very detailed data. With regard to seasonality, given the fact that we do not have any panel data and that within each survey year all households have been interviewed during the same period, there is no convincing method to accurately quantify the seasonal effect on expenditure declarations.

To redress the problem of a recall and/or disaggregation bias, it is sometimes suggested to only include those consumption items in the household expenditure aggregate which were unaffected by changes in the recall period and/or the disaggregation of consumption items (Deaton and Drèze, 2002; Tarozzi, 2004; Lanjouw and Lanjouw, 2001). However, the application of the above suggested method would have meant in both cases to exclude basic food items which account for a very large share of total Burkinabè household expenditure. Moreover, this method introduces a new bias if the budget share devoted to the 'excluded' consumption items changes over time, which is likely given the strong annual and seasonal price fluctuations of basic food items.

Last, whereas the proposed methods do certainly improve poverty estimates whenever only one of the above described changes in survey design is relevant, we think that given the various changes in survey design in Burkina Faso, any corrections would not only have tremendously decreased the transparency of the poverty estimates but would even have led to a further enhancement of measurement error.

We therefore decided to compute the expenditure aggregate - which will be presented in Section 1.4.1 - without any further corrections for survey design. But we will check the robustness of our poverty estimates in Sections 1.4.2. Another alternative would have been to exclude the household survey of 1994 and only use the surveys of 1998 and 2003, which have a much higher degree of comparability (Table 1.2). But we think all information available should be used to analyze not only short-term but also long-term growth and poverty dynamics in Burkina Faso.

## 1.4 Revised Growth-Poverty Assessments

### 1.4.1 Revised Poverty and Inequality Estimates

Using a time consistent expenditure aggregate and poverty line, but making no corrections for changes in household survey design, we provide a new poverty and inequality assessment for Burkina Faso in Table 1.4. According to these new estimates, national headcount poverty, or P0 of the FGT measures (Foster et al.,

1984), increased strongly between 1994 and 1998 from 55.5 to 61.8 percent but then decreased, also substantively, between 1998 and 2003 to 47.2 percent, i.e. to a lower level than in 1994. In rural areas, we find the same poverty dynamics, but on a higher level: from 63.4 in 1994 to 68.7 in 1998 to 53.3 percent in 2003. In urban areas, we show that poverty increased from 14.7 in 1994 to 27.3 in 1998 and then decreased to 20.3 percent in 2003. Therefore, and in contrast to rural areas, urban poverty in 2003 was still substantially higher than in 1994, indicating an 'urbanization of poverty' (see also Haddad et al., 1999). But throughout all three survey years poverty in urban areas remained significantly lower than in rural areas.

Table 1.4: Poverty and Inequality Trends - Revised Estimates

| | Urban | | | Rural | | | National | | |
|---|---|---|---|---|---|---|---|---|---|
| | 1994 | 1998 | 2003 | 1994 | 1998 | 2003 | 1994 | 1998 | 2003 |
| P0 | 14.7 | 27.3 | 20.3 | 63.4 | 68.7 | 53.3 | 55.5 | 61.8 | 47.2 |
| P1 | 3.9 | 8.3 | 5.7 | 24.1 | 25.8 | 18.3 | 20.9 | 22.9 | 16.0 |
| P2 | 1.5 | 3.5 | 2.3 | 11.7 | 12.5 | 8.3 | 10.0 | 11.0 | 7.3 |
| Gini | 0.45 | 0.50 | 0.48 | 0.39 | 0.35 | 0.39 | 0.47 | 0.45 | 0.45 |
| PL | | 1994 | | | 1998 | | | 2003 | |
| CFA F (Index 1994=100) | | 53,219(100) | | | 82,885(155.7) | | | 82,672(155.3) | |

*Source:* EPI, EPII, EPIII. Computations by the authors.
*Notes:* P0: poverty headcount. Gini: measure of inequality. The revised national poverty lines (PL) are calculated by the authors and expressed on a yearly per capita basis in current CFA F. The Gini coefficient is population weighted.

Between 1994 and 1998, inequality as measured by the Gini coefficient increased from 0.45 to 0.50 in urban areas, but decreased from 0.39 to 0.35 in rural areas and from 0.47 to 0.45 on a national level. Thereafter between 1998 and 2003, inequality stagnated in urban areas, increased again to 0.39 in rural areas, but remained constant on a national level, indicating a compensation of higher within group inequality by lower between group (urban/rural) inequality.

Obviously, this new assessment sheds a totally different light on poverty dynamics in Burkina Faso during the last ten years (see Tables 1.1 and 1.4). Whereas official estimates showed - more or less - stagnant national poverty rates, the revised poverty rates indicate rising poverty between 1994 and 1998 and falling poverty thereafter, with poverty in 2003 being below poverty in 1994. An interesting question is which of the biases described and corrected had the largest impact on the difference between original and revised estimates. Table 1.5 therefore provides the quantitative impact of the various adjustments made.

Table 1.5: Decomposition of the Bias in Official Poverty Estimates

| | Survey Year | | |
|---|---|---|---|
| | 1994 | 1998 | 2003 |
| *P0 (official estimates)* | *44.5* | *45.3* | *46.4* |
| Consistent Welfare Aggregates | | | |
| Hypothetical Rents | 41.2 | (45.3) | (46.4) |
| Exclusion of Durables | (41.2) | 45.8 | 47.2 |
| No Adjustment to NA | (41.2) | 53.6 | (47.2) |
| Consistent Poverty Lines | | | |
| Constant Consumption Basket | 55.5 | 61.8 | (47.2) |
| *P0 (revised estimates)* | *55.5* | *61.8* | *47.2* |
| Consistent Survey Design | | | |
| Survey period pre-harvest | increase | 61.8 | 47.2 |
| Recall period 15 days | decrease | 61.8 | 47.2 |
| 80 expenditure items | decrease | 61.8 | 47.2 |

*Source:* EPI, EPII, EPIII. Computations by the authors.
*Notes:* Parentheses indicate that no change occurs with respect to the previous estimate. The decomposition would slightly differ if the poverty line was changed before the re-computation of the expenditure aggregate.

It can be seen that the consistent inclusion of hypothetical rents considerably reduces poverty in 1994. The complete exclusion of durables has only a minor impact, but somewhat increases poverty in 1998 and 2003. As one can expect, omitting the 'correction factor' of 1.124 in 1998 substantially increases poverty in 1998, namely by 7.8 percentage points. In other words, the computation of a consistent expenditure aggregate already leads to a considerable increase in poverty between 1994 and 1998 and to a decrease between 1998 and 2003. But poverty in 2003 would still be higher than poverty in 1994. Only the use of a time-consistent poverty line leads to a poverty reduction between 1994 and 2003.

As described in Section 1.3.3, we did not correct for changes in survey design between 1994 and 1998/2003 because an exact quantification of the bias linked to survey design doesn't seem to be possible. Hence, in Table (1.5) we only indicate if corrections for biases in survey design would in- or decrease our poverty estimates in 1994 and provide a robustness check of our revised poverty trends in next section.

### 1.4.2 Robustness Check

To assess the robustness of our results, we first provide a rough monetary quantification of the biases induced by changes in survey design between 1994 and 1998/2003. Second, we confront our estimated poverty trends with a dynamic wellbeing assessment based on several non-monetary indicators.

With regard to seasonality, if we rely on a study by Reardon and Matlon (1989) who have shown for the case of poor households in Burkina Faso that consumption varies by about 13 percent across seasons, we may assume that real expenditures in the pre-harvest season in 1998/2003 were on average not more than 13 to 15 percent underestimated in comparison to 1994.

With regard to the longer recall period in 1994, if we take a study of Deaton (2003a) who has shown an increase of 30 percent declared expenditure for a decrease in the recall period from 30 to 7 days, we estimate that the recall bias might be responsible for about 11 percent higher declared consumption in 1998/2003 compared to 1994. More precisely, if a decrease in the recall period from 30 to 7 days leads to 30 percent higher declared expenditure, a decrease from 30 to 15 days should not lead to a higher than 15 percent increase in declared expenditure.[13] As only food expenditures, which account for not more than 70 percent of households' expenditure in Burkina Faso, were affected by the change in recall period, we calculate 0.7 times 0.15 which is equal to about 11 percent.

Last, we address the bias that might be induced by a higher disaggregation of expenditure items between 1994 and 2003. A study by Lanjouw and Lanjouw (2001) indicates an increase of declared expenditure of 0.05 percent for every 'per-

[13] We can assume that the bias is less severe for longer recall periods.

cent' consumption item added.[14] Applying these estimates to the case of Burkina Faso, suggests that consumption in 1998 and 2003 was overestimated by about 2 (1998) and 3 (2003) percent, respectively (in comparison to 1994).

Notice that the above biases in survey design offset each other to a large extent. More precisely, whereas the pre-/post-harvest bias underestimates consumption in 1998/2003 by about 13 to 15 percent, the bias in the recall period overestimates consumption in 1998/2003 by 11 percent and the number of declared consumption items overestimates consumption in 1998/2003 by 2 to 3 percent, in comparison to 1994. This implies that our poverty estimates should be quite accurate with regard to poverty trends.

Moreover, only if consumption *increased* across all households by more than 12 percent in 1998, the poverty headcount in 1998 would be lower than the poverty headcount estimated for 1994. Conversely, only if consumption *decreased* across all households by more than 17 percent in 2003, the poverty headcount in 2003 would be higher than the poverty headcount estimated for 1994. In other words, the pre-/post-harvest bias would have to off-set the two later biases by more than 12 percent in consumption to obtain a poverty headcount for 1994 which is higher than the one estimated for 1998. Conversely, the latter two biases would have to offset the pre-/post-harvest bias by more than 17 percent in consumption to offset the stated poverty reduction between 1994 and 2003.

Both scenarios are very unlikely given the approximated biases induced by changes in survey design. Therefore, the finding that poverty increased between 1994 and 1998 and decreased between 1994 and 2003 (and hence also between 1998 and 2003) seems quite robust against these three sources of bias in survey design.

Next, we compare our monetary estimates with various non-monetary indicators of wellbeing. As shown in Table 1.6 our revised assessment of monetary poverty is also in line with the development of various social indicators. These measures were computed with the same household surveys, but were not subject to potential seasonal, recall, or disaggregation biases in survey design, nor were they affected by an 'arbitrary' poverty line - or difficulties in adjusting poverty

[14]This is an average estimate for the poorest 50 percent of the population. Lanjouw and Lanjouw (2001) show that the bias induced by a disaggregation of expenditure items rather decreases for households at the upper end of the expenditure distribution.

Table 1.6: Non-Monetary Indicators of Wellbeing

| | Urban | | | Rural | | | National | | |
|---|---|---|---|---|---|---|---|---|---|
| | 1994 | 1998 | 2003 | 1994 | 1998 | 2003 | 1994 | 1998 | 2003 |
| Education | | | | | | | | | |
| Illiteracy rate | 51.1 | 51.2 | 46.1 | 89.4 | 89.1 | 88.9 | 82.7 | 81.8 | 79.6 |
| Enrolled 6 to 18 | 62.2 | 60.2 | 64.3 | 21.9 | 16.5 | 19.9 | 28.0 | 23.4 | 27.5 |
| Health | | | | | | | | | |
| Handicap | 4.8 | 5.9 | 2.4 | 5.1 | 5.7 | 2.7 | 5.1 | 5.9 | 2.9 |
| Med. Consult | 45.9 | 50.9 | 71.2 | 37.1 | 42.0 | 60.7 | 39.5 | 44.2 | 63.0 |
| Housing | | | | | | | | | |
| Electricity | 29.7 | 35.7 | 45.6 | 0.7 | 0.4 | 1.0 | 5.4 | 6.3 | 9.3 |
| Water | 23.5 | 24.0 | 27.1 | 0.3 | 0.1 | 0.2 | 4.1 | 4.2 | 5.2 |
| Sanitation | 88.8 | 84.8 | 90.8 | 18.1 | 14.6 | 21.3 | 29.5 | 26.3 | 34.2 |

*Source*: EPI, EPII, EPIII. Computations by the authors.
*Notes:* Illiteracy rate: Share of illiterate individuals older than 18 years. Enrolled 6 to 18: Share of children 6 to 18 years old enrolled in school. Handicap: Share of individuals living in a household where the household head suffers from a handicap. Med. Consult: Share of ill persons having consulted medical services. Electricity, Water, Sanitation: Share of individuals living in a household with access to modern energy, water, and sanitation facilities.

lines over time. Notice that non-monetary indicators usually provide a more long-term trend in changes in poverty as they are much more stable over time and are less prone to annual wellbeing fluctuations. Moreover, improvements in non-monetary welfare indicators are - at least in the short and medium term - infrequently reversed in case of economic downturns.

Enrollment rates in urban as well as in rural areas decreased between 1994 and 1998 and increased between 1998 and 2003. The share of persons living in a household where the household head suffers from a serious physical handicap increased between 1994 and 1998 and decreased afterwards. Whereas living conditions, for example electricity connection or a comfortable access to (proper) water or toilet facilities, did not improve much between 1994 and 1998 or even deteriorated,[15] they improved substantially between 1998 and 2003. All non-monetary

[15]One might question whether housing is at all able to deteriorate, i.e. if a household already connected to modern electricity, water and sanitation facilities can be disconnected over time. However, whether a household uses modern electricity, water and sanitation facilities does not only depend on the access to the infrastructure but also on the ability to pay for user fees and

indicators, except, interestingly, school enrollment in rural areas,[16] show also improvements between 1994 and 2003.

These results support our estimated monetary poverty dynamics of increasing poverty between 1994 and 1998 and decreasing poverty thereafter, as well as an overall poverty reduction between 1994 and 2003. It might be worthwhile to mention that non-monetary indicators are certainly not a perfect indicator of changes in money-metric poverty of individual households (e.g. Klasen, 2000). However, in the long run and on an aggregate (i.e. national) level the correlation between these two dimensions of poverty is in general quite high (e.g. Kanbur and Squire, 2001). We analyzed a rather short period of 9 years and hence the previous statement does not fully apply. But we can at least state that social indicators showed the same trends as our monetary poverty estimates between 1994 and 2003.

### 1.4.3 Growth Elasticities of Poverty

Based on our revised estimates we analyze in more detail the link between macroeconomic growth and micro-economic poverty reduction, calculating growth elasticities of poverty[17] for selected monetary and non-monetary welfare indicators. The growth elasticity of poverty $\varepsilon$ simply calculates the relative change in poverty given a one percent increase in GDP per capita between $t$ and $t-1$. For the case of the headcount poverty $P0$ this implies:

$$\varepsilon_t = \frac{\Delta P0_{t,t-1}/P0_{t-1}}{\Delta GDP_{t,t-1}/GDP_{t-1}} \tag{1.1}$$

where $P0$, the headcount poverty, can refer to any monetary or non-monetary indicator. It has been argued that for policy purposes the impact of growth in GDP per capita on *absolute* changes in poverty (and not *relative* changes in poverty)

maintenance, which may indeed decrease over time. Moreover, Burkina Faso faced very high population growth rates, with an average of 2.4 percent per year in the last decade. If hence no improvements in infrastructure take place, high population growth can easily lead to a decrease of infrastructure access per capita. Last, migration is a widespread phenomenon in Burkina Faso and it is thus also likely that families move to poorer housing (with less infrastructure) if their economic situation worsens.

[16]The decrease in rural enrollment rates is obviously also reflected in national enrollment rates.

[17]Additional measures to assess the impact of growth on poverty, or in other words to assess the 'pro-poorness' of growth, are presented in Essay 2.

might be more relevant (Klasen and Misselhorn, 2006). Hence, alternatively we compute the growth semi-elasticity of poverty given by:

$$\varepsilon_t = \frac{\Delta P0_{t,t-1}}{\Delta GDP_{t,t-1}/GDP_{t-1}} \tag{1.2}$$

Instead of analyzing the impact of GDP growth per capita on poverty changes, one might think of using the Gross National Income (GNI) per capita instead. As income flows in- and out of the country are rather low for Burkina Faso, the difference between the two is, however, quite small: between 1994 and 2003 the growth rate of GDP per capita was 2.30 percent, whereas the growth rate of GNI per capita amounted to 2.34 percent (World Bank, 2005). Alternatively, also the mean income as measured in the household surveys could be applied as a denominator in equation (1.1) and (1.2). But as all three Burkinabè household surveys, EPI, EPII, and EPIII, only contain reliable information on households' consumption and not on income,[18] calculated growth elasticities of poverty would more or less only yield the distributional change in consumption of households. Thus we only report GDP growth elasticities of poverty.

For the case of Burkina Faso, as one can expect from the previous section, the monetary growth elasticity of poverty, was positive between 1994 and 1998 and negative between 1998 and 2003 and between 1994 and 2003. More precisely, between 1994 and 1998 a one percent growth of GDP per capita on the national level was accompanied by a 0.9 percent increase in the poverty headcount index. In contrast, between 1998 and 2003 the respective elasticity was -2.9, showing that during that later period macro-economic growth led to strong poverty reduction. In total, this lead to an overall weak growth elasticity of poverty of -0.8 over the whole period 1994-2003 (Table 1.7).

In rural areas, the elasticities were in all periods very close to the national ones, namely 0.7 for 1994-1998, -2.7 for 1998-2003, and -0.9 for 1994-2003.[19]

[18] As in most developing countries, with a large rural population mainly living from subsistence farming, expenditures rather than income is the better measure of households' monetary well-being (see e.g. Deaton, 1997 for discussion), LSMS household surveys usually focus on a precise data collection of expenditures rather than of income.

[19] One should rather state that the national elasticities were very close to the rural elasticities as national elasticities are driven by rural elasticities with about 80 percent of the Burkinabè population living in rural areas (Günther and Grimm, 2004).

Table 1.7: Selected Growth Elasticities of Poverty

| | 1994-1998 | | | 1998-2003 | | | 1994-2003 | | |
|---|---|---|---|---|---|---|---|---|---|
| | Urban | Rural | National | Urban | Rural | National | Urban | Rural | National |
| | | | | Growth Elasticities | | | | | |
| Expenditure | 6.8 | 0.7 | 0.9 | -3.2 | -2.7 | -2.9 | 1.6 | -0.9 | -0.8 |
| Health | 1.8 | 1.2 | 1.2 | -5.2 | -14.6 | -6.3 | -1.6 | -2.5 | -2.3 |
| Education | 0.4 | 0.5 | 0.5 | -1.3 | -0.5 | -0.7 | -0.3 | 0.1 | 0.0 |
| Water | 0.0 | 0.0 | 0.0 | -0.5 | 0.0 | -0.1 | -0.3 | 0.0 | -0.1 |
| Sanitation | 2.8 | 0.3 | 0.4 | -4.9 | -1.1 | -1.3 | -1.0 | -0.2 | -0.4 |
| | | | | Growth Semi-Elasticities | | | | | |
| Expenditure | 1.0 | 0.4 | 0.5 | -0.9 | -1.2 | -1.8 | 0.3 | -0.5 | -0.4 |
| Health | 0.1 | 0.1 | 0.1 | -0.3 | -0.4 | -0.4 | -0.1 | -0.1 | -0.1 |
| Education | 0.2 | 0.4 | 0.4 | -0.5 | -0.4 | -0.5 | -0.1 | 0.1 | 0.0 |
| Water | 0.0 | 0.0 | 0.0 | -0.3 | 0.0 | -0.1 | -0.2 | 0.0 | -0.1 |
| Sanitation | 0.3 | 0.3 | 0.3 | -0.7 | -0.8 | -1.0 | -0.1 | -0.2 | -0.3 |

*Source:* Poverty Estimates: EPI, EPII, and EPIII. Computations by the authors. GDP per capita growth rates: IAP.
*Notes:* Expenditure: Change in share of individuals living below the poverty line specified in Section 1.4.1. Education: Change in share of individuals aged 6-18 not enrolled in school. Health: change in share of individuals living in a household where the household head suffers from a severe handicap. Water and Sanitation: Share of individuals living in a household with poor water or sanitation facilitates.

In urban areas, the respective elasticities were 6.8 (1994-1998), -3.2 (1998-2003), and 1.6 (1998-2003). Hence, urban elasticities were usually higher in magnitude than rural and national elasticities, and growth led - again in contrast to the rural and national level - to a poverty *increase* over the whole observation period.

Comparing these growth elasticities of poverty with non-monetary elasticities, it is first of all interesting to see that non-monetary elasticities are most of the time - but not always - positively correlated with monetary growth elasticities of poverty (Table 1.7). Furthermore, the extent as well as the variation over time of elasticities is much lower for non-monetary than for monetary indicators. This seem to indicate both that there is some inertia in non-monetary welfare changes - whether this is positive or negative from a normative perspective is not clear - and that the correlation between macro-economic growth and non-monetary poverty is in general lower than between growth and monetary poverty.

Last, the comparison with growth semi-elasticities shows that when comparing elasticities across space and across indicators, semi-elasticities seem to be more relevant than elasticities (Table 1.7). As elasticities are largely driven by the initial poverty level, with lower poverty levels leading to higher growth elasticities (Klasen and Misselhorn, 2006), the impact of growth on poverty seems to be overestimated for areas and indicators with low poverty levels. Using semi-elasticities instead of elasticities leads to much more similar results across space (urban, rural, national) and welfare indicators (expenditure, health, education, and housing). Obviously, the differences across time remain whether we use elasticities or semi-elasticities.

## 1.5 Conclusion

### 1.5.1 The 'Arithmetic' Paradox

Previous poverty assessments for Burkina Faso neglected some important methodological inconsistencies with regard to the measurement of poverty dynamics and led to the so-called 'Burkinabè Growth-Poverty-Paradox' between 1994 and 2003, i.e. relatively sustained macro-economic growth, but stagnating poverty rates despite constant inequality estimates. Addressing these methodological inconsistencies (see Section 1.3) by calculating a time consistent welfare aggregate and welfare cutoff, we show that poverty actually decreased between 1994 and 2003. Hence, and in contrast to previous studies, we state that growth was actually pro-poor, i.e. growth of GDP per capita led to poverty reduction, with a growth elasticity of poverty close to -1.

Several methodological conclusions can be drawn from these revised results. First, this analysis has clearly shown that poverty rates might be considerably driven by the methodology used to compute the poverty line and welfare aggregate as well as by survey design, which can significantly lower the comparability of poverty estimates across time. Burkina Faso is certainly no exception here and methodological differences or inconsistencies might explain a considerable part of the observed heterogeneity of growth elasticities of poverty across countries.

This also implies that a continuous quality improvement of household surveys, which is done in many developing countries, might lead to better *static* poverty estimates but might lead to considerable biases in estimated poverty *trends*. Hence, there might be some trade-off between estimating state-of-the-art poverty 'snap-shots' or poverty 'dynamics'.

Moreover, the scientific debate on robust poverty estimates over time often focuses on the impact of the initial location of poverty lines on calculated poverty dynamics (see e.g. Davidson and Duclos, 2000). However, as already argued by Lanjouw (1998) the vigorous attention paid to a 'precise' location of a poverty line might be misplaced. Poverty lines will always retain an element of arbitrariness. Instead, it might be worthwhile to pay more attention to a 'precise' inflation of poverty lines.

Last, we have shown, that growth elasticities of non-monetary poverty can help to 'verify' money-metric growth elasticities of poverty. Non-monetary indicators are less prone to time-inconsistent surveys, data, and poverty lines, and are hence more comparable over time as well as across countries. These indicators have however rarely been used in the literature on cross-sectional growth elasticities of poverty.[20] Calculating non-monetary growth elasticities of poverty might also be interesting for projections in the context of the Millennium Development Goals (MDGs). Observed monetary growth elasticities of poverty have often been used to forecast the progress towards MDG One[21] (for an overview see Rami, 2006). No such analysis has yet been done for the other seven MDGs which are based on non-monetary welfare indicators.

### 1.5.2 The 'Economic' Paradox

We redress the 'Burkinabè paradox' between 1994 and 2003 and show that growth indeed led to poverty reduction. However, we now show that poverty even *increased* despite macro-economic growth between 1994 and 1998, and in urban areas also between 1994 and 2003. Whereas we redress the 'paradox' between 1994 and 2003 from an *arithmetic* perspective, we can *explain* the remaining 'paradox' between 1994 and 1998 (and between 1994 and 2003 in urban areas) from an *eco-*

[20] One exception is e.g. a study of Grosse et al. (2006), which uses non-monetary indicators for a pro-poor growth assessment of Bolivia based on the growth incidence curve (see also Essay 2).

[21] MDG One: Eradicate extreme hunger and poverty. Target One: Reduce by half the proportion of people living on less than a dollar a day.

*nomic* perspective: by addressing variations in the purchasing power of the poor relative to the non-poor.[22]

The poverty up-swing between 1994 and 1998 can be explained by a considerable increase in food prices after one of the severest Burkinabè droughts in 1997/98, primarily increasing the cost-of-living of the poor.[23] This led to the massive inflation of the poverty line relative to the CPI between 1994 and 1998 (Figure 1.3 and Table 1.4). The reason why growth did not even lead to poverty reduction between 1994 and 2003 in urban areas can again be explained by changes in the purchasing power of the urban (poorer) population. The devaluation of the CFA-Franc in 1994, which on the one hand led to gains in competitiveness of Burkinabè enterprises, led on the other hand to a significant decrease in the purchasing power of the employed urban population, as wages were not indexed to inflation after the devaluation (for details see Grimm and Günther, 2004).

These results nicely demonstrate that the general trend in Burkina Faso of macro-economic growth leading to poverty reduction has been interrupted twice by economic shocks which had a considerable impact on poverty. From 1994 onwards the urban poor population was severely affected by the devaluation of the CFA-Franc and in 1998 one of the most devastating Burkinabè droughts had a massive impact on rural poverty rates. Hence, the impact of (reoccurring) shocks (and not only policies) on the heterogeneity of growth elasticities of poverty should receive further attention.[24]

Last, the estimated different growth elasticities of poverty across time and space also clearly illustrate that long-term trends on the national level might cover huge spatial and temporal disparities. Thus, as the relationship between growth and poverty can enormously vary over time and space, average growth elasticities of poverty can be quite misleading even for a single country let alone for all countries (see e.g. Ravallion and Chen, 1997; Ram, 2006).

---

[22] A more detailed analysis of the impact of changes in relative purchasing power on pro-poor growth (assessments) is provided in Essay 2.

[23] Due to the fact, that on an annual basis more than 70 percent of farmers in rural areas are net buyers and not net sellers of food crops, even most of the households engaged in food crop production could not benefit from the price increase after the drought.

[24] See also Essay 3 for a detailed discussion on the impacts of shocks on poverty dynamics.

# Essay 2

# Pro-Poor Growth and Inflation Inequality

*The essence of money is in its absolute worthlessness.*
Norman O. Brown, 1913-2002

**Abstract:** Despite the extensive debate on how to define and measure pro-poor growth, neither the theoretical literature on pro-poor growth nor empirical applications have paid sufficient attention to inflation inequality, or in other words to varying inflation rates across the income distribution. We show that incorporating inflation inequality into pro-poor growth measures is not only a theoretical necessity but if ignored can seriously bias empirical assessments of the pro-poorness of growth. Hence, we suggest simple methods to redress such bias. As an empirical illustration, we apply our concepts to the case of Burkina Faso, using the growth incidence curve and the decomposition of poverty changes as pro-poor growth measures.

---

based on joint work with Michael Grimm.

## 2.1 Introduction

Pro-poor growth (PPG), i.e. the question to what extent the poor benefit from economic growth, has over the past years become one of the central issues of development economics. Also in this context, the question of how one should define and measure pro-poor growth has been intensively discussed and a wide range of definitions and measures of pro-poor growth have been provided by several authors.[1]

Despite the ongoing debate on the concept and measurement of PPG, there is especially one point that has not received sufficient attention in all PPG measures - or at least in their respective applications: the issue of inflation inequality, i.e. the phenomenon of substantially varying inflation rates across households along the income distribution. The existence of inflation rates which differ by household income is very well supported by various studies for both industrialized countries (e.g. Slesnick, 1993; Newbery, 1995; Crawford and Smith, 2002; Hobijn and Lagakos, 2003) as well as developing economies (e.g. Pritchett et al., 2000; Deaton, 1998; Deaton, 2003a). Moreover, the issue of varying inflation rates should receive particular attention in the measurement of PPG, given that these dynamic welfare measures are especially focused on disaggregated growth rates, or in other words, on the change of purchasing power across the *entire* income distribution.

For all that, PPG measures usually assume away inflation inequality and only use aggregate (national) price indices to deflate income over time. If, however, the aspect of inflation inequality is ignored - independent of which definition or measurement of pro-poor growth is used - we might not derive an appropriate assessment of whether and to what extent the poor benefited from economic growth, i.e. to what extent growth was 'pro-poor'.

The objective of this paper is, hence, first to demonstrate *theoretically* how inflation inequality can easily be incorporated into any PPG measures, using the *Growth Incidence Curve* (Ravallion and Chen, 2003) and the *Datt-Ravallion Decomposition of Poverty Changes* (Datt and Ravallion, 1992) as two widely used measures. Second, we illustrate *empirically*, for the case of Burkina Faso, how

[1] For a comprehensive overview and comparison of the various measures see e.g. Son (2003a) or Klasen (2004).

pro-poor growth assessments can differ whether the phenomenon of inflation inequality is taken into account or not.

The remainder of the paper is organized as follows. Section 2.2 briefly reviews the different concepts and measures of pro-poor growth. Section 2.3 discusses the phenomenon of inflation inequality, or in other words income-correlated inflation rates, both from a theoretical as well as from an empirical perspective. Section 2.4 first outlines the standard methods to construct growth incidence curves and to perform poverty change decompositions and second, suggests for both approaches alternative methods which take into account inflation inequality. Section 2.5 illustrates the importance of using these adjusted PPG measures for the case of Burkina Faso. Section 2.6 concludes.

## 2.2 Measurements of Pro-Poor Growth

Almost all of the numerous PPG measures are on the one hand built on one of two broader 'conceptional' categories, and on the other hand, on one of two broader 'methodological' categories.

Concerning the two 'conceptional' categories, one can distinguish between an 'absolute' concept and a 'relative' concept of pro-poor growth. The former 'absolute' concept defines growth to be pro-poor if growth leads to absolute poverty declines, irrespective of whether inequality in- or decreases (e.g. Kraay, 2003; Ravallion, 2004). The latter 'relative concept' only classifies growth to be pro-poor if the poor benefit relatively more than the average or the non-poor from economic growth, i.e. growth has to be accompanied by decreasing inequality (e.g. Kakwani and Pernia, 2000; Klasen, 2004).

In addition to this 'conceptional' difference, PPG measures might also be subdivided into two 'methodological' categories. 'Growth patterns' analyze the changes in income over the whole or part of the income distribution, i.e. they compute income-specific disaggregated growth rates to analyze which segments of the income distribution benefited most from growth: examples are the distribution-weighted growth rate of Klasen (1994), the poverty growth curve of Son (2003b) and the growth incidence curve of Ravallion (2004). The advantage of these measures is that they do not need to specify a poverty line and that changes in the income of the poorest of the poor can be taken into account. A problem with those measures is that they are sometimes not able to provide a clear index if a certain growth process was more pro-poor than another.

The second 'methodological' group might be called 'growth-poverty-links'. All of these measures link in some way or the other changes in poverty to changes in mean income and/or to changes in inequality: examples are the decomposition of poverty of Datt and Ravallion (1992), the poverty bias of growth of McCulloch and Baulch (2000) and the poverty equivalent growth rate of Kakwani and Pernia (2000). The advantage is that, in contrast to 'growth patterns', these measures are able to provide a specific pro-poor growth *index*, which facilitates pro-poor growth comparisons across countries and time. The problem is that they are based on country-specific poverty lines which make the outcome of such measures very sensitive to the poverty line chosen and to the country's initial income distribution and initial level of economic development (see Bourguignon, 2003).

Obviously, whether and to what extent a specific growth process[2] was pro-poor might in a lot of cases be assessed differently by the various PPG measures - depending on which concept and method they are based on. But diverging results should not lead to the conclusion that a certain PPG assessment is not robust to different measures or that some measures do not capture pro-poor growth appropriately. In contrast, different concepts and methods look at pro-poor growth from different perspectives, and taken together help to get a more detailed and comprehensive picture. Different measures should therefore be considered as complements rather than as substitutes.

There is, however, one issue that all PPG measures have in common, no matter if they are based on the 'absolute' or 'relative' concept of pro-poor growth or if they fall into the category of 'growth patterns' or 'growth-poverty-links'. They all consider pro-poor growth as a function of growth rates among the poor. Certainly, here the *real* increase in purchasing power among the poor and not nominal growth rates are of interest, leading to the essential question which price deflator should be used to compare incomes over time. In most applications of PPG measures the general (national) Consumer Price Index (CPI) is used for this purpose, which might in many cases, and as shown in next section, not be an appropriate deflator for all income groups.

[2]In general, one is interested in a particular country over a specific period of time.

## 2.3 Theory and Empirics of Inflation Inequality

### 2.3.1 Homogenous Price Indices

Whenever we are interested in the evolution of households' wellbeing over time, i.e. in *real* changes of wellbeing or utility, *nominal* income changes have to be deflated with an appropriate deflator which should ideally represent the change in the cost-of-living of households, defined as:

$$COL_t = \frac{e(u, p_t)}{e(u, p_{t-1})} \tag{2.1}$$

where $e(u, p)$ is the minimum expenditure required to reach the utility level $u$, given prices $p$. It is hardly feasible to calculate such a cost-of-living index, which could also be labeled as an *utility index*. The utility derived from different consumption baskets is not observable and even the calculation of a simple ordering of utilities would require knowledge of preferences, whose approximation would imply some 'arbitrary' assumptions (Deaton and Zaidi, 2002). Moreover, we might also not have prices and measured quantities for all goods being part of a household's utility function.

Hence, as a short-cut a *price index*, which is in general the Consumer Price Index (CPI), is applied as an approximate estimate, to derive *real* changes of households' wellbeing over time. The CPI measures the change in prices over time paid by an 'average' household for a specific and constant consumption basket:

$$CPI_t = \frac{\sum_{j=1}^{J} p_{t,j} q_{t-1,j}}{\sum_{j=1}^{J} p_{t-1,j} q_{t-1,j}} \tag{2.2}$$

where $p_{t,j}$ is the price and $q_{t,j}$ the quantity consumed of good $j$ at time $t$. As can be seen from equation (2.2), the CPI usually constitutes a Laspeyres index, i.e. the quantities $q$ of the base period $t-1$ are held constant. The quantities $q_{t-1}$, or more often the weights $w_{t-1}$[3], of the consumption basket are either derived from the aggregate expenditure shares of the National Accounts or Household Surveys, or from the expenditure shares of specially designed 'Price and Expenditure Surveys'.

[3] $w_{t-1,j}$ is the expenditure share $\frac{p_{t-1,j} q_{t-1,j}}{\sum_{j=1}^{J} p_{t-1,j} q_{t-1,j}}$ of good $j$.

Obviously, such a CPI does not account for differences in the consumption pattern of different households. Moreover, and what is most interesting for pro-poor growth analysis, because of the averaging process in its construction, the CPI usually gives more weight to the consumption pattern of rather 'rich' households, bypassing the consumption pattern of the majority of the poorer population (see e.g. Prais, 1959; Nicholson, 1975; Ley, 2005).[4]

If the CPI is computed via National Accounts or Household Surveys this is simply due to the fact that expenditures of richer households are much higher than those of poorer ones. Therefore the expenditure shares of richer households largely determine the aggregate weights for each consumption item. This means that the CPI is not based on a 'democratic' basis, where each household's expenditure shares would get an equal weight, but on a 'plutocratic' basis where households are weighted according to their total expenditure. Hence, although the budget shares of the CPI are equal to the budget shares of an 'average' or an 'aggregate' household they are not 'representative' for the majority of households (Ley, 2005).

If specific 'Price and Expenditure Surveys' are used, in general, still more weight is given to the consumption pattern of rather rich households. Because of data availability, especially in developing countries, often only urban households working in the 'formal' sector are surveyed.[5] These households are very likely to be situated at the upper-end of the income distribution.

This bias would obviously not matter if there was no systematic relationship between total household expenditure and the expenditure pattern of households. However, households with lower income are very likely to have consumption patterns that differ significantly from households with higher income (see Section 2.3.2). The general CPI is therefore usually very close to a price index computed specifically for the 'rich' but is significantly different from a price index specifically computed for the poor.[6] Thus Arrow (1958) stated already in the 1950s that 'there should be a separate cost-of-living index number for each income level'.

[4]Clearly, there are several other reasons, why the CPI does not reflect the 'true' price index of various households. For an overview see for example Boskin et al. (1997) or Lebow et al. (2003).

[5]See also Essay 4 on a detailed discussion of 'informal' and 'formal' employment.

[6]For example, Deaton (1998) estimates for the US that the budget shares in the CPI are representative for households at the 75th percentile of the expenditure distribution.

Whereas this is sometimes recognized in industrialized countries, where price indices are computed for several income groups, this is only rarely done in developing countries, but should not be of less importance here (see e.g. Guénard, 1998; Pritchett et al., 2000a; Deaton, 2003b).

## 2.3.2 Heterogenous Consumption Patterns and Prices

In general, it can be assumed that households with lower income spend relatively more on necessities, whereas relatively well-off households spend more on luxury goods (see e.g. Arrow, 1958 or Engel's Law). In developing economies, one of the most important difference between poor and non-poor households' expenditure pattern is the share of total income spent on food (Deaton, 1997).

As food represents the 'first necessity' of a household's consumption, poor households spend the highest share of their income on food items. In addition, the demand for food items is characterized by rather low income elasticities. Hence, the household budget share devoted to food expenditures substantially decreases with increasing total income.[7] This relationship between total household income and the allocation of household resources between food and non-food items was already analyzed in the early economic literature (Engel, 1895) and became known as the *Engel curve*, which states that the food share in total consumption decreases as total expenditure increases.

Certainly, differences in the consumption pattern between poor and non-poor households alone would not lead to different inflation rates, as long as the various goods households consume showed equal price movements. However, if this were the case we would not even need to construct a CPI: if it were assumed that all price movements were highly correlated over time, simply the price change of *one* consumption good would have to be measured. And in developing countries, particularly the prices of domestically produced food crops are often only weakly correlated with general price movements (see e.g. Pritchett et al., 2000a; Marouani and Raffinot, 2004).

[7]At the very low end of the income distribution this might not necessarily be the case (e.g. Deaton and Paxson, 1998) with higher income leading to higher food consumption and to a (more expensive) dietary change.

Food production is, especially in sub-Saharan Africa countries, to a large extent heavily dependent on annual fluctuations of climatic conditions and - compared to other sectors - less dependent on long-term macro-economic policies.[8] Moreover, these countries often face significant transport and trade constraints. Thus, a lower domestic production of food crops cannot easily be substituted with higher imports of food crops, which could *in theory* smooth food supply and prices.

Also, (basic) food items do not only account for a larger share in poor households' budget, but poor households have in general rather limited substitution possibilities for (basic) food items. If the relative price of food increases, food can only be substituted up to a minimum of about 2100 calories per person with non-food items. If the *relative* price of *basic* food items increases, again poor households can only to a certain extent substitute *basic* food items with *absolutely* more expensive food items.[9] This might lead to very low price elasticities of demand for basic food items. Hence, in the presence of low income elasticities as well as low price elasticities of food demand, food production fluctuations can lead to considerable food price swings and to considerable inflation differences across the income distribution.

Given the fact that all pro-poor growth measures are interested in the change of the purchasing power of the poor, using the CPI seems therefore not very appropriate. Instead, price indices, which are relevant to the poor (and non-poor) should be used. This is true for both PPG measures which analyze the growth rate along the income distribution as well as for PPG measures which focus on changes in poverty rates (see Section 2.2).

For a methodological and empirical illustration of how inflation inequality can be considered in PPG measures, the *Growth Incidence Curve* (GIC), as proposed by Ravallion and Chen (2003), and the *Decomposition of Poverty Changes*, as suggested by Datt and Ravallion (1992), will be applied. The former falls into the 'methodological' category of 'growth patterns' and the latter into the category of

[8]See also Essay 1 and Essay 3.

[9]A closely related issue is raised in the entitlement approach of famines (Sen, 1981).

'growth-poverty-links'. Both can assess whether and to what extent growth was 'absolutely' and 'relatively' pro-poor.[10]

## 2.4 Methodology

### 2.4.1 Growth Incidence Curve with PCPIs

The growth incidence curve (GIC), as proposed by Ravallion and Chen (2003), calculates the growth rate in income per capita (or alternatively the growth rate in expenditure per capita) at each percentile point along the income distribution. The GIC is hence defined as:

$$g_{t(p)} = \frac{y_{t(p)}}{y_{t-1(p)}} - 1 \tag{2.3}$$

where $g_{t(p)}$ is the growth rate in income $y$ of the $p$th percentile between $t$ and $t-1$. If the GIC is positive at all points up to some point $z$, then poverty, as measured by the Watts index (Watts, 1968), has fallen for all poverty lines up to $z$ and hence growth has been pro-poor up to point $z$. The extent of the pro-poorness of growth, or the rate of pro-poor growth, is defined as the area under the GIC up to point $z$. Thus growth is obviously more pro-poor if the GIC shifts upward at all points along the income distribution up to point $z$.

The GIC and the thereof derived rate of pro-poor growth first of all focuses on the absolute income growth of the poor. However, the GIC also allows conclusions on the relative extent to which growth was pro-poor, i.e. if the poor benefited relatively more than the average or non-poor from economic growth. Such an analysis can be undertaken, by comparing the ***mean of the percentile-specific growth rates***, which is defined as:

$$g_{p,t} = \frac{1}{100} \sum_{p=1}^{100} g_{t(p)} \tag{2.4}$$

with the ***growth rate in mean income***, which can be written as:

$$g_{\mu,t} = \frac{\mu_t}{\mu_{t-1}} - 1 \tag{2.5}$$

[10] An additional motivation to use these two measures for illustrative purposes is that both are now widely used by international organizations in the current assessment of the pro-poor growth performance of developing countries (see e.g. the *Operationalizing Pro-Poor-Growth* (OPPG) project sponsored and managed by the World Bank).

where $\mu_t$ is the mean income of the whole income distribution at time $t$. Whenever the growth rate in equation (2.4), which is population weighted and hence gives more weight to the income growth of the poor, is higher than the growth rate in equation (2.5), which is expenditure weighted, and thus often largely determined by growth gains of the richest two quintiles (Klasen, 1994), growth can be considered to be pro-poor in relative terms. Alternatively, the shape of the GIC can be analyzed: If the GIC is downward sloping over the whole income distribution then the distributional pattern of growth benefited the poor, whereas if the GIC is upward sloping over the whole income distribution the upper end of the income distribution benefited relatively more from economic growth.

Equation (2.3) represents the GIC in nominal terms. In empirical analysis, we are, however, interested in real and not nominal percentile-specific growth rates. Applications of the GIC, therefore, usually compute:

$$g_{t(p)} = \frac{y_{t(p)} \cdot \frac{1}{1+i_t}}{y_{t-1(p)}} - 1 \qquad (2.6)$$

where $i_t$ is the inflation rate approximated by the national CPI between $t$ and $t-1$. Such an approach would only be justified if the inflation rate was the same for all percentiles across the income distribution. However, and as argued in Section 2.3, this is often not the case. CPIs are generally much closer to a computed price index for the non-poor and might be significantly different from a computed price index for the poor.

Using a price index, which is for most households not representative, as a deflator to compare incomes over time is certainly less problematic if applied to national means, i.e. to equation (2.5). In contrast, if the effort is made to calculate *percentile-specific* incomes with micro-economic household survey data, we should also use *percentile-specific* consumer price indices (PCPIs) for the computation of *percentile-specific* growth rates. Otherwise, we are not only inconsistent in our methodological approach, but might also draw wrong conclusions about the 'pro-poorness' of growth, both from an absolute and a relative perspective. The GIC should therefore be calculated as:

$$g_{t(p)} = \frac{y_{t(p)} \cdot \frac{1}{1+i_{t(p)}}}{y_{t-1(p)}} - 1 \qquad (2.7)$$

where $i_{t(p)}$ is the specific inflation rate of the $p$th percentile, which should be approximated by PCPIs, which take into account the specific consumption basket of the households at the $p$th percentile at time $t$.

Certainly, one might argue that PCPIs are also misleading because they implicitly assume that there is no mobility across the income distribution. However, GICs and hence also PCPIs rely on the axiom of anonymity, i.e. they only compare cross-section distributions (and not panel distributions) ignoring mobility of households along the income distribution. This means that the percentile-specific income, and hence also the percentile-specific consumer price indices, should only be seen as representative for specific percentiles and not of specific households within these percentiles. The underlying assumption is that the consumption pattern of households is largely determined by income and that households with certain not income-related preferences for specific consumption baskets do not systematically move through the income distribution over time.[11] However, it would certainly be interesting to calculate GICs with PCPIs for panel data.

### 2.4.2 Triple Decomposition of Poverty

The decomposition of poverty changes over time as proposed by Datt and Ravallion (1992) analyzes the contribution of (i) changes in mean income and (ii) changes in income inequality to changes in poverty over time. Hence, two components are calculated: (i) the change in poverty that would have emerged if the observed growth rate had occurred without any changes in inequality and (ii) the change in poverty that would have occurred if the observed changes in inequality happened in the absence of growth in mean income (see Figure 2.1). This can be written as:

$$\Delta P_{t+1,t} = [P(\mu_{t+1}, L_t) - P(\mu_t, L_t)] + [P(\mu_t, L_{t+1}) - P(\mu_t, L_t)] + R_{t+1,t} \quad (2.8)$$

where $P(\mu_t, L_t)$ is the poverty measure with a mean income of $\mu_t$ and a Lorenz curve $L_t$ in period $t$. The first component of equation (2.8) corresponds to the

[11] In fact we do control for rural and urban residence - as the consumption pattern of rural and urban households in developing countries is in general quite different - and calculate price indices separately for rural and urban households.

change in poverty explained by the growth component with a constant relative income distribution while the second component corresponds to the change in poverty explained by the distribution effect (see also Figure 2.1).

Figure 2.1: Decomposition Paths of Poverty

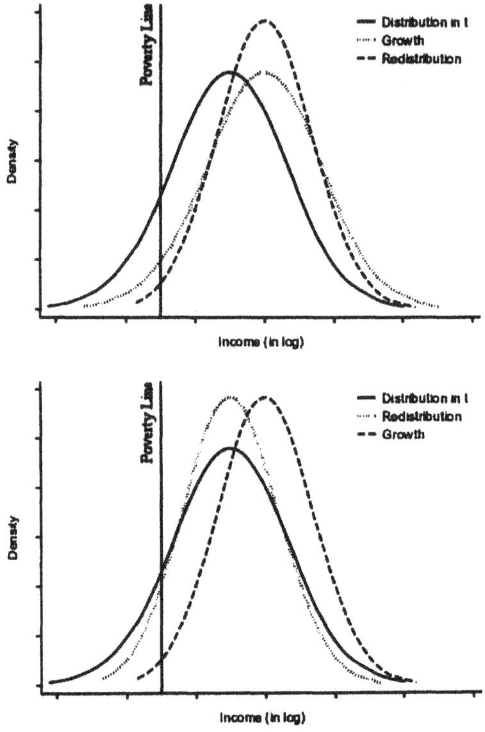


*Source:* Own Illustration.
*Notes:* – Income distribution in year $t$ ($\mu_t, L_t$). - - - Income distribution in year $t$+1 ($\mu_{t+1}, L_{t+1}$). Grey line: Decomposition path (upper graph: $\mu_{t+1}, L_t$, lower graph: $\mu_t, L_{t+1}$).

The magnitude of both components is path dependent, i.e. depends on whether first the growth and then the distribution component or vise versa is computed. This is nicely illustrated in Figure 2.1. In both graphs the solid black line represents the income distribution in period *t*. However, whereas in the first graph the growth component is followed by the redistribution component, in the second graph the redistribution components is followed by the growth component, which, as can be seen in Figure 2.1, has an impact on the size of the respective components.

Because of this path dependency, the magnitude of the growth and redistribution components in equation (2.8) is dependent on whether the initial or the final year is taken as the reference period.[12] Moreover, whenever we use the initial (or final) period to compute both the growth and the redistribution components, we also obtain a residual $R$, which represents the interaction term between the growth and distribution components. Hence, in many empirical applications, first the initial and then the final year is taken as a reference period and then the decomposition results are averaged over the two possible reference years. This methodology provides the averages of the growth and redistribution components and cancels out the residuals.

Such a decomposition of observed poverty changes obviously requires that the poverty line is kept constant in real terms over time. This means, that the inflation rate underlying the poverty line should be equal to the inflation rate underlying the income variables, which is in general the CPI. As discussed in Section 2.3, the consumption basket underlying the poverty line should in general be quite different from the one underlying the CPI and thus the implicit inflation rate of the poverty line might be substantially different from the inflation rate of the CPI. This can lead to a poverty line in $t+1$ whose real value in terms of purchasing power has remained constant but whose 'real' value in relation to a hypothetically CPI inflated poverty line has considerably changed.

This means, that besides a growth and a redistribution component, we have to compute a third component when decomposing poverty changes: a 'relative price shift' or 'poverty line' component (see Figure 2.2), which is the change in poverty explained by the difference of the inflation rate of the poverty line to the inflation rate of the general CPI, or in other words, the change in poverty explained by a relative price shift between the bundle of goods consumed by the poor and the

[12] In equation (2.8) the initial year $t$ is taken as the reference period.

bundle of goods consumed by the non-poor. We therefore derive the following 'triple' poverty decomposition:

$$\Delta P_{t+1,t} = [P(\mu_{t+1}, L_t, z_t) - P(\mu_t, L_t, z_t)] + [P(\mu_t, L_{t+1}, z_t) - P(\mu_t, L_t, z_t)] + [P(\mu_t, L_t, z_{t+1}) - P(\mu_t, L_t, z_t)] + R_{t+1,t} \quad (2.9)$$

Similar to a dual decomposition, the first component corresponds to the change in poverty explained by the growth component (with a constant real poverty line) and the second component corresponds to the change in poverty explained by the distribution effect (again with a constant real poverty line). The third component now corresponds to the change in poverty explained by relative price changes, i.e. caused by the inflation difference between the poverty line and the national CPI, in a growth- and distributional neutral case. $R$ is again the residual.

Figure 2.2: Triple Decomposition of Poverty

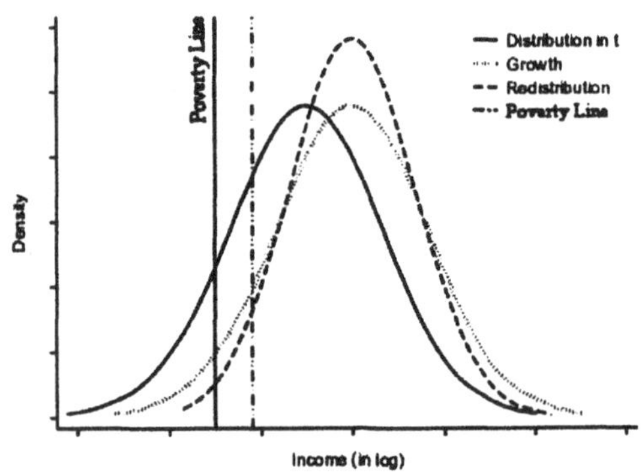


*Source:* Own Illustration.
*Notes:* – Income distribution in year $t$ ($\mu_t, L_t$). - - - Income distribution in year $t$+1 ($\mu_{t+1}, L_{t+1}$).

As already discussed, in a dual decomposition of poverty changes decomposition results are averaged over the two reference periods $t$ and $t+1$ to derive the 'average' growth and distribution components as well as to cancel out the residual. Note that in a dual decomposition taking the initial and final year as reference points to calculate the growth and redistribution component is equal to computing all growth and redistribution fragments of the $2! = 2$ possible decomposition paths.

In a triple decomposition 'only' taking the average over the components computed in the initial and the final year is somewhat arbitrary as several of the growth, redistribution, and poverty line fragments of the now $3! = 6$ possible decomposition paths are left out.[13] More precisely, the intermediate step of any triple decomposition path is ignored. Hence, we propose that in a triple decomposition all six decomposition paths are calculated to derive the average growth, inequality and poverty line components. By doing so, also the residual is canceled out. A STATA 8.0 Macro to undertake such a 'triple' decomposition can be found in Appendix A.

To derive the impact of the change in the poverty line relative to the CPI, the poverty line $z_{t+1}$ is calculated by deflating the 'real' poverty line in $t+1$ with the change of the CPI between $t$ and $t+1$. Hence, if the implicit inflation rate of the poverty line were the same as the CPI the calculated poverty line $z_{t+1}$ would be equal to the poverty line $z_t$, and the 'poverty line' component would cancel out.

Two points are worth to note. First, in this 'triple' decomposition the growth (and inequality) component has to be interpreted a bit differently than in a 'dual' decomposition. It represents the change in poverty that would have occurred with the observed growth rate (change in inequality) given that all households had experienced the same change in the 'cost-of-living', or in other words, given that the consumption basket underlying the poverty line had experienced the same increase in prices than the consumption basket underlying the CPI.

Second, although closely related to the adjustments made for inflation inequality in the calculation of growth incidence curves, here instead of percentile-specific inflation rates only two different inflation rates are taken into account: one for the poor (represented by the implicit inflation rate of the poverty line) and one for the non-poor (represented by the CPI). One might think about applying percentile-specific price indices for the deflation of households' consumption. The growth component of such a triple decomposition would then constitute the growth component taking into account differences in inflation rates across households, whereas the inequality component would show the 'real' and not 'nominal' change in inequality across time. Instead of the CPI, a 'democratic' price index, which is the average of the percentile-specific price indices, should be applied to

[13] For example in Figure 2.2 only one, namely the growth-redistribution-poverty line decomposition path, of 6 possible decomposition paths is illustrated.

deflate the 'real' poverty line in $t+1$. The interpretation of such a poverty line component, which should be quite small, is however not clear.

We do not opt for this latter approach because of two reasons. First, the latter approach does not clearly show the impact of inflation inequality on changes in poverty, as relative price shifts are partly captured by the growth component, partly captured by the inequality component, and partly captured by the poverty line component. Hence, the first method mentioned is much more transparent. Second, as in some countries it might be quite difficult to derive percentile-specific price indices, we think that a triple decomposition of poverty which only requires the CPI and the implicit inflation rate of the poverty line is often much more feasible. Such a triple decomposition does therefore also present a nice alternative to the growth incidence curve whenever we are interested in pro-poor growth measures which are sensitive to inflation inequality.

## 2.5 Empirical Application

### 2.5.1 Data Description

We take the case of Burkina Faso during the period 1994 to 2003 to empirically illustrate the implication of inflation inequality adjusted growth incidence curves and poverty decompositions. The analysis is based on three household surveys, *Enquêtes Prioritaires* (EP), which were all undertaken by the *Institut National de la Statistique et de la Démographie* (INSD) with the financial and technical assistance of the World Bank in 1994 (EPI), 1998 (EPII), and 2003 (EPIII). The respective sample sizes are 8,642, 8,478, and 8,500 households. All three surveys contain detailed information on disaggregated expenditure data of households which are necessary both to calculate households' expenditure per capita[14] as well as percentile-specific inflation rates (PCPIs). For a more detailed discussion of the data see also Grimm and Günther (2004).

To estimate PCPIs, we first calculate for each household in the household survey of 2003 the budget shares for the seven expenditure categories represented in

[14]Note that for an empirical application we use expenditure and not income to assess households' welfare, which is the preferred welfare measure for households in developing countries (Deaton, 1997; Deaton and Zaidi, 2002).

Table 2.1: Household Expenditure Budget Shares

| | Budget Shares | | |
|---|---|---|---|
| | CPI | 1st Dec. | 10th Dec. |
| Food Crops | 0.10 | 0.36 | 0.12 |
| Other Food Items | 0.24 | 0.30 | 0.27 |
| Rent and Utilities | 0.11 | 0.22 | 0.15 |
| Education | 0.03 | 0.01 | 0.02 |
| Health | 0.04 | 0.01 | 0.06 |
| Transport | 0.16 | 0.00 | 0.07 |
| Transfers | 0.00 | 0.00 | 0.06 |
| Others | 0.33 | 0.10 | 0.25 |
| Total | 1.00 | 1.00 | 1.00 |

*Source:* Consumer Price Index (CPI): *Institut National de la Statistique et de la Démographie* (INSD). Household Budget Shares: EPIII. Computations by the authors.

the CPI.[15] Table 2.1 shows the average budget shares of the first and last decile in the Burkinabè household expenditure distribution, also in comparison with the respective expenditure weights used in the national CPI. As can be seen, the main difference between poor and rich households' expenditure pattern is the share of income spent on staple food. Food crops add up to almost 40 percent of total expenditure for the poorest households, but account for only 12 percent of expenditure for the very rich.

It is striking, that the expenditure share for food crops in the CPI is even smaller than of the richest 10 percent of the expenditure distribution. This shows that the CPI in Burkina Faso is not only income-biased but also urban-biased. Whereas the expenditure shares of the CPI were derived from an 'Expenditure Survey' of formal urban households in 1998 (INSD 1998) the expenditure shares for the richest 10th percent of the expenditure distribution is computed for the entire population. Not only poorer but also rural households spend a relatively higher share on food crops.

Second, we analyzed the price changes for the main staple foods (maize, millet, sorghum, and rice) in Burkina Faso between 1994 and 2003. The prices were

[15] The seven expenditure categories in the Burkinabè CPI are food crops, other food items, rent and utilities, education, health, transport, and others.

taken from the Burkinabè *Grain Market Price Surveillance System* (Ministry of Trade, Burkina Faso, 2004), which collects prices of the major cereals on various regional markets in Burkina Faso on a weekly basis. A food crop price index was computed as a weighted average of the prices paid for maize, millet, sorghum, and rice, using the weights applied by the INSD to compute the food poverty line in Burkina Faso in 2003.

As documented in Table 2.2, the prices of these goods of first necessity increased much faster than those for most other goods between 1994 and 2003. Whereas the CPI only increased by 31.4 percent, the prices for food crops increased by 125.2 percent during the same period.[16]

Table 2.2: National Price Indices

| | 1994 | 2003 |
|---|---|---|
| CPI | 100.0 | 131.4 |
| Food Crops | 100.0 | 225.2 |
| CPI w/o Food Crops | 100.0 | 121.0 |

*Source:* Consumer Price Index (CPI): INSD. Food Crops: *Burkinabè Grain Market Price Surveillance System*. CPI w/o Food Crops: Computation by the authors.

Combining the results of Table 2.1 with the once of Table 2.2, one can easily derive PCPIs which take into account the specific consumption pattern of households and the relative price change between staple foods and other consumption goods that occurred in Burkina Faso between 1994 and 2003. More precisely, first, the average budget shares for food crops and 'other consumption goods' over expenditure percentiles were computed for 2003. Second, these shares were used as weights for the computation of percentile-specific price indices, accounting for the specific price changes of food crops, as measured by the *Grain Market Price*

[16]This massive price distortion mainly occurred between 1994 and 1998, when the CPI increased by only 22.7 percent but food crop prices increased by 152.2 percent. Conversely, between 1998 and 2003, the CPI continued to rise whereas prices for food crops decreased (see also Grimm and Günther (2004) and Essay 1).

*Surveillance System* and of 'other consumption items', as measured by the CPI with the price change of food crops netted out (Table 2.2).[17]

Given the illustrative purpose of this analysis we only distinguished between food crops and 'other consumption items'. Of course one could be more specific and distinguish between the eight expenditure categories as outlined in Table 2.1 and thus derive even more refined household deflators. However, since the main difference in consumption patterns as well as in relative price changes were between staple foods and other goods (see Tables 2.1 and Table 2.2), this simplified approach should be sufficient to demonstrate the impact of inflation inequality.[18]

Note that in contrast to the CPI which represents a Laspeyres index, we used a Paasche index[19] to construct the PCPIs. In general, the Paasche index reflects a lower-bound whereas the Laspeyres index reflects an upper-bound to the 'true' change in cost-of-living, as they both do not allow for substitution, i.e. they ignore the fact that consumers adjust their consumption basket when relative prices change.[20]

Mainly because of practical reasons, the CPI is often a Laspeyres index as it requires lower data requirements (Boskin et al., 1997). For the Laspeyres index 'old' budget shares can be applied, whereas for the Paasche index the budget shares of the 'current' period need to be calculated. We applied a Paasche index, to be consistent with the estimated poverty lines, which are also based on a

[17]Obviously, such price information from government price surveys is not a perfect data source and one would prefer price information directly observed in household surveys. But given the fact that in the Burkinabè household surveys, households only reported total expenditures for each consumption category, and no information on quantities or prices was given, these prices were the only available to us.

[18]Moreover, most of the other expenditure categories in the CPI represent very heterogeneous categories. For example, transport expenditures among rich households might be composed of quite different expenditure items than among poor households and we do not possess price deflators which are more disaggregated than general 'transport expenditure'.

[19]A Laspeyres index calculates the price changes between $t$ and $t+1$ of an observed consumption basket of the base period $t$. In contrast, in a Paasche index, the observed consumption basket of the final period $t+1$ is held constant.

[20]Or in other words, the Laspeyres index might overstate inflation rates and understate increases in wellbeing, whereas the Paasche index might understate inflation rates and overstate increases in wellbeing.

Paasche index.[21] Moreover, the expenditure shares of the official CPI of Burkina Faso were derived from an 'Expenditure Survey' which was undertaken in 1998 (INSD, 1998). Thus using the expenditure shares of the EPIII in 2003 is not 'less appropriate' than using the expenditure shares of the EPI in 1994. In any case, we also applied a Laspeyres instead of a Paasche index for a robustness check. This did not significantly alter the estimated PCPIs. Since in Burkina Faso the substitution of food crops is - as expected - rather low, the difference between a Laspeyres and a Paasche index is not too large.

Since we can only observe budget shares and not quantities in the household surveys we have to rewrite the Paasche index at a specific percentile $p$ along the income distribution as:

$$P_{t(p)} = \frac{\sum_{j=1}^{J} p_{t,j} q_{t(p),j}}{\sum_{j=1}^{J} p_{t-1,j} q_{t(p),j}} = \left[ \sum_{j=1}^{J} w_{t(p),j} \frac{p_{t-1,j}}{p_{t,j}} \right]^{-1} \tag{2.10}$$

where $p_{t,j}$ is the price of good $j$ at time $t$. $q_{t(p),j}$ would be the quantity consumed at the $p$th percentile. But since we cannot observe $q_{t(p),j}$ with our household surveys, we use $w_{t(p),j}$ as the share of households' total budget devoted to item $j$.

Figure 2.3, which indicates the price index between 1994 and 2003 for each percentile of the expenditure distribution and separately for rural and urban areas, clearly shows that the cost-of-living of the poor increased much faster than of the non-poor, leading to a redistribution of purchasing power in favor of the rich, which is not appropriately reflected in the general CPI. Also the prices of the rural population increased much more than of the urban population.[22]

The poverty lines for 1994, 1998, and 2003, necessary for the decomposition of poverty changes, were constructed as described in Essay 1. As discussed, they also constitute a Paasche index.

[21] The reason why the poverty line we use is based on a Paasche index is to be in line with the latest official poverty estimates in Burkina Faso (see Essay 1).

[22] Note that before applying the PCPIs to deflate household expenditures, we also adjusted household expenditures for price differences among the 13 Burkinabè regions. These deflators were provided by the INSD in Burkina Faso. These deflators are sought to reflect general regional price differences, but do not take into account differences in consumption habits of households.

Figure 2.3: Price Indices Curves

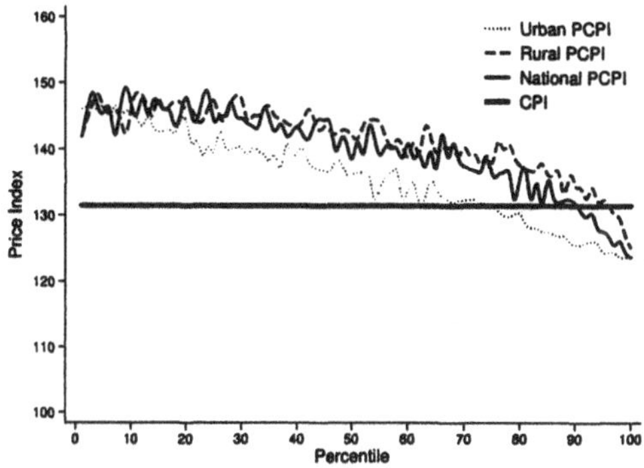


*Source*: EPI, EPIII. Computations by the authors.
*Notes*: The price indices in 1994 is set to 100.

### 2.5.2 Growth Incidence Curve with PCPIs

Figure 2.4 shows the national growth incidence curve, the growth rate in mean, and the mean of percentile-specific growth rates computed with both the general Burkinabè CPI and with PCPIs from 1994 to 2003. Figures 2.5 and Figure 2.6 show the same curves separately for urban and rural households. If we first take a look at the GICs, where the general CPI was used to convert nominal into real household expenditure per capita (represented by the grey lines in Figures 2.4, 2.5, and 2.6), we observe that household per capita expenditure increased to a significant extent over the whole income distribution on the national as well as on the rural level but not in urban areas.

Hence, on the national level as well as in rural areas, growth was absolutely pro-poor independent of where the poverty line is set, as both the national and rural GIC is above zero for all percentiles of the expenditure distribution. In contrast, in urban areas growth is only slightly pro-poor up to the 20th percentile, then up to the 80th percentile growth rates are negative but then again positive thereafter. Also, the mean of the percentile-specific growth rates lies above the growth rate in mean for both the national and the rural level, whereas the contrary is true for urban areas. This indicates that national and rural growth (in contrast to urban

Figure 2.4: Growth Incidence Curves - National

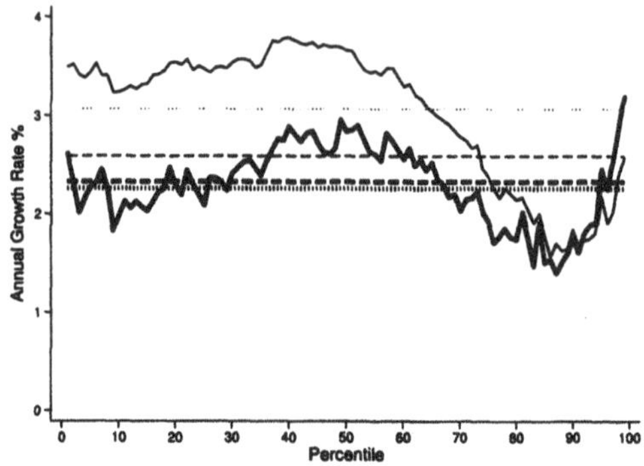


*Source:* EPI, EPIII. Computations by the authors.
*Notes:* All growth rates correspond to annualized growth rates (in %) of household per capita expenditure. — Growth incidence curve. - - - Growth rate in mean. ··· Mean of percentile-specific growth rates. Thin lines: CPI as deflator. Thick lines: PCPIs as deflators.

growth) was also pro-poor taking the relative concept of pro-poor growth, i.e. the poor benefited relatively more than the average from economic growth (see also Table 2.3).

Analyzing the growth incidence curves which use PCPIs as a deflator (represented by the black lines in Figures 2.4, 2.5, and 2.6) it can clearly be stated that growth in Burkina Faso between 1994 and 2003 was less pro-poor both in absolute and in relative terms than it was suggested by the CPI-deflated GICs. Among poor households in both rural and urban areas, the percentile-specific growth rates computed with the PCPIs are substantially lower than those computed with the CPI. The difference is, as expected, considerably smaller among urban households and for households at the upper part of the income distribution, reflecting the fact that their specific consumption pattern is much closer to the weights underlying the CPI (Table 2.1).

Moreover, growth in Burkina Faso was not only in absolute but especially in relative terms less pro-poor if the more appropriate PCPIs are applied. With the PCPIs the mean of the percentile specific growth rates lies below the growth rate in mean for national, urban, and rural households. This implies that the poor

Figure 2.5: Growth Incidence Curves - Urban

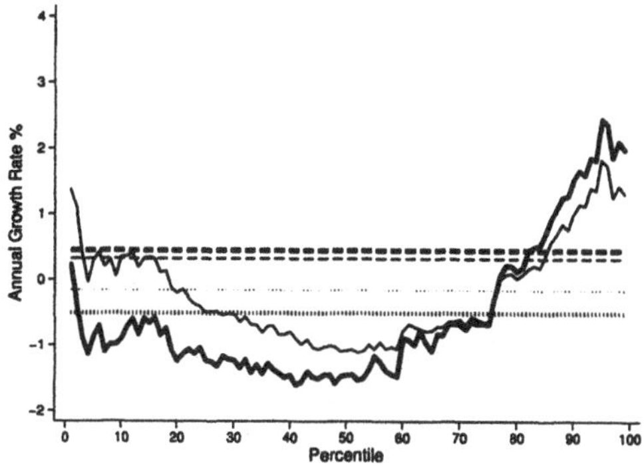


Figure 2.6: Growth Incidence Curves - Rural

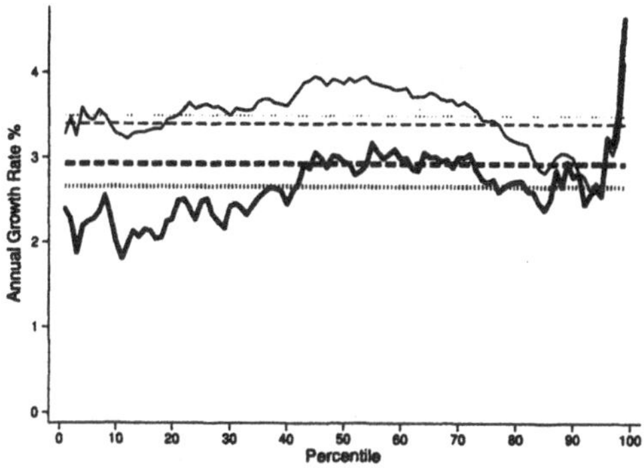


*Source:* EPI, EPIII. Computations by the authors.

*Notes:* All growth rates correspond to annualized growth rates (in %) of household per capita expenditure. — Growth incidence curve. - - - Growth rate in mean. ··· Mean of percentile-specific growth rates. Thin lines: CPI as deflator. Thick lines: PCPIs as deflators.

benefited relatively less than the average population from growth. This stands in contrast to the empirical results derived with the CPI-deflated GICs, where the poor (at least on the national and rural level) seemed to have benefited more than the non-poor from economic growth (see also Table 2.3).

Table 2.3: Growth Rate in Mean & Mean of Growth Rates

| | | Urban | Rural | National |
|---|---|---|---|---|
| CPI | $g_\mu$ | 0.3 | 3.4 | 2.6 |
| | $g_p$ | -0.2 | 3.5 | 3.1 |
| PCPIs | $g_\mu$ | 0.5 | 2.9 | 2.3 |
| | $g_p$ | -0.5 | 2.6 | 2.3 |

*Source:* EPI, EPIII. Computations by the authors.
*Notes:* CPI: Growth rates calculated with the general consumer price index. PCPIs: Growth rates calculated with percentile-specific price indices. $g_\mu$: Growth rate in mean. $g_p$: Mean of percentile-specific growth rates. All growth rates are annual growth rates in household expenditure per capita.

Comparing growth rates in mean and means of percentile-specific growth rates calculated with the general CPI on the one and calculated with PCPIs on the other hand also nicely illustrates that applying the CPI as a deflator to national averages is less problematic than to income level specific growth rates. As expected, growth rates in mean income computed with the CPI and PCPIs are much closer than the means of percentile-specific growth rates (Table 2.3).

If we focus on the shape of the curves, we see that in contrast to the CPI-deflated GICs now all PCPIs deflated curves show a massive 'up-swing' of growth rates at the upper-end of the income distribution, implying that, due to their specific consumption pattern, households along the upper percentiles of the income distribution were less affected by the massively increasing food prices between 1994 and 2003, and hence gained in relative purchasing power. This loss of relative purchasing power of the poor is not appropriately reflected in the GICs if the CPI is used as a deflator.[23]

[23] Note that the use of PCPIs does *not* necessarily lead to GICs that are less pro-poor than GICs calculated with the general CPI. At least for the case of Burkina Faso, the different inflation rates we could observe across the income distribution were not correlated over time. This means that percentiles which experienced higher than average inflation rates than others in one period (1994-1998) did not necessarily face higher than average inflation rates in the next period (1998-2003).

### 2.5.3 Triple Decomposition of Poverty

Table 2.4 (a) and Figure 2.7 show the estimates of a 'triple' decomposition of poverty changes. As can be seen in Table 2.4 (a) and Figure 2.7, the impact of the 'poverty line' component on changes in poverty can be significantly negative (between 1994 and 1998 and between 1994 and 2003) as well as positive (between 1998 and 2003) and might in some cases even outweigh the impact of the growth as well as the redistribution component. This implies that relative price changes were the major force behind the poverty increase which could be observed between 1994 and 1998. In addition, poverty would have decreased by 17.5 percent between 1994 and 2003 if the prices of the goods of the poor had experienced the same inflation rates as the prices of the goods of the non-poor. However, the high relative price shifts offset the positive effects of the growth and redistribution component by 9.2 percentage points (Table 2.4 (a)).

Figure 2.7: Poverty Decomposition of ΔP0

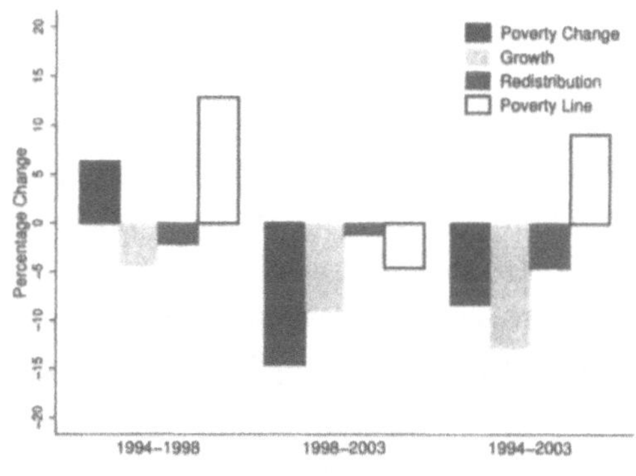


*Source:* EPI, EPII, EPIII. Computations by the authors.
*Notes:* Illustrated impacts correspond to Table 2.4.

Such a 'triple' decomposition seems not only useful whenever the development of the price index specific to the consumption of the poor differs significantly from the development of the general CPI, but also for long term poverty decompositions. Several authors have stated that in the course of economic development it is very unlikely that the poverty line can be kept absolutely constant over time,

Table 2.4: Poverty Decomposition of ΔP0

| Year | 1994-1998 | 1998-2003 | 1994-2003 |
|---|---|---|---|
| ΔP0 | 6.3 | -14.6 | -8.3 |
| (a) Growth (CPI) | -4.4 | -9.0 | -12.9 |
| Redistribution | -2.2 | -1.2 | -4.6 |
| Poverty Line (PLPI) | 12.9 | -4.6 | 9.2 |
| *Residual* | 0 | 0 | 0 |
| ΔP0 | 6.3 | -14.6 | -8.3 |
| (b) Growth (PLPI) | 8.6 | -13.3 | -3.5 |
| Redistribution | -2.3 | -1.3 | -4.8 |
| Poverty Line (PLPI) | 0 | 0 | 0 |
| *Residual* | 0 | 0 | 0 |
| ΔP0 | -8.8 | -9.9 | -18.6 |
| (c) Growth (CPI) | -4.8 | -10.3 | -13.4 |
| Redistribution | -4.0 | 0.4 | -5.2 |
| Poverty Line (CPI) | 0 | 0 | 0 |
| *Residual* | 0 | 0 | 0 |

*Source:* EPI, EPII, EPIII. Computations by the authors.
*Notes:* CPI: consumer price index used as a deflator. PLPI: poverty line price index used as a deflator.

even if the objective is to measure absolute poverty (see e.g. Kilpatrick, 1973; Jäntti and Danziger, 2000). Since even the concept of *absolute* poverty cannot be seen independently of the social and economic development of a country, significant economic progress usually leads to a real increase of poverty lines. Hence, and for a better understanding of the driving forces behind changes in poverty, it should be useful to include a 'relative price shift' or 'poverty line component' into decompositions of poverty changes in any case.

Or, to be consistent with the 'dual' decomposition methodology, as proposed by Datt and Ravallion (1992), one has to make sure that the poverty line is kept constant in real terms over time, which means that the income variable and the poverty line have to be de- or inflated with the same price index.

This can either be achieved by using the inverse of the implicit inflation rate of the poverty line between $t$ and $t+1$ as a deflator for the income variable at $t+1$ (Table 2.4 (b)), maintaining the purchasing power of the poverty line but deflating all incomes with the inflation rate of the poor. Obviously, the change in poverty is the same as in a triple decomposition (Table 2.4 (a)). The growth component of this decomposition reflects the poverty change explained by the growth of the purchasing power of the poor (Table 2.4 (a)). Hence, it captures approximately the growth and the poverty line or price shift component of a triple decomposition.

An alternative is to inflate the poverty line in year $t$ of the base year with the inverse of the deflator which is used to deflate the income variable in year $t+1$. Table 2.4 (c) shows that if the poverty line is inflated over time with the CPI, we obtain estimated poverty changes which are quite different to the poverty in- or decreases stated with a triple decomposition. This is caused by a change in the underlying real purchasing power of the poverty line, as the CPI often under- or overstates the change in cost-of-living of the poor. Note that in such a dual decomposition the growth and redistribution component are very similar to a triple decomposition, whereas the poverty change captures the 'real' change in poverty and the poverty line or price shift component of a triple decomposition.

Both described alternative methods obviously lead to a poverty line component which is equal to zero and hence constitute a 'dual' decomposition

## 2.6 Conclusion

As relative price shifts between goods primarily consumed by the poor and goods primarily consumed by the non-poor often constitute an important phenomenon of developing countries, we argued both from a theoretical as well as from an empirical perspective that inflation inequality has to be included in PPG measures.

Since all PPG measures intend to measure the impact of economic growth on the *real* and not *nominal* income growth of the poor (often relative to the non-poor), PPG measures should use appropriate and distinctive price deflators for the poor and the non-poor. Hence, we proposed simple methods how inflation inequality can be incorporated into PPG measures.

We further illustrated that these alternative methodologies are not only of theoretical relevance, but that they might also significantly alter our perception of the participation of the poor in economic growth. For the case of Burkina Faso between 1994 and 2003, we showed that 'ignoring' relative price changes can considerably bias pro-poor growth measures.

We think that from a methodological perspective, this paper can be a useful contribution to the measurement of pro-poor growth, as the issue of inflation inequality across income groups, although widely recognized, has so far been ignored in these types of dynamic welfare measures. Certainly, one might question whether 'more than one price index number can be tolerated without confusion' (Prais, 1958). However, we think that in case of large income (and hence also consumption pattern) disparities, as they persist in developing countries, and in case where we are interested in growth rates across the entire income distribution and not only in the growth rate in mean, 'complexity' should rule over 'simplicity'.

This paper might therefore also add to the extensive literature on whether a 'plutocratic' or a 'democratic' price index is appropriate for the measurement of wellbeing over time (for an overview see e.g. Ley, 2005). We have shown that even if from a macro-perspective the difference of the two indices might in some cases be rather small (which would justify applying a simpler and more transparent 'plutocratic' price index), the difference can still be substantial from a micro-perspective.

From a policy perspective, our findings have clearly shown that only if we consider the changes in the cost-of-living of the poor relative to the non-poor, we appropriately measure how successful countries were in achieving pro-poor growth. In addition, when estimating the pro-poorness of certain policies, besides their impact on economic growth and inequality, their impact on relative price changes should also be carefully analyzed. Last, from an empirical perspective, including the aspect of inflation inequality in PPG measures might also considerably alter the obtained results from cross-country PPG studies.

# Essay 3

# Vulnerability to Idiosyncratic and Covariate Shocks

*Prediction is very difficult, especially about the future.*
Niels Bohr, 1885 - 1962

**Abstract:** Households in developing countries are frequently hit by severe idiosyncratic and covariate shocks leading to high consumption volatility. A household's currently observed poverty status might therefore not be a good indicator of the household's general poverty risk or vulnerability. Although several measures to analyze vulnerability have recently been proposed, empirical studies are still rare as the data requirements for these measures are often not met. In this paper, we propose a simple method to empirically assess the impact of idiosyncratic and covariate shocks on households' vulnerability, which can be applied in a wide context as it relies on commonly available living standard measurement surveys. We empirically illustrate our approach for Madagascar and show that covariate shocks have a comparatively higher impact on rural households' vulnerability whereas idiosyncratic shocks have a comparatively higher impact on urban households' vulnerability.

---

based on joint work with Kenneth Harttgen.

## 3.1 Introduction

Households in developing countries are frequently hit by severe idiosyncratic and covariate shocks resulting in high income volatility.[1] Although (poor) households in risky environments have developed various ex-ante and ex-post risk-coping strategies to reduce income fluctuations or to insure consumption against these income fluctuations, the variance of households' consumption over time remains generally high (see e.g. Townsend, 1994; Udry, 1995). A household's currently observed poverty status is, therefore, in many cases not a very good guide for a household's vulnerability to poverty, i.e. its general poverty risk. Or in other words, whereas some households are trapped into chronic poverty, others are only temporarily poor, whereas other households, currently non-poor, might still face a high risk to fall into poverty in the future.

Most established welfare measurements, e.g. the FGT poverty measures (Foster et al., 1984), only assess the current poverty status of households, ignoring poverty dynamics. Results from such a static poverty analysis might therefore be misleading if high consumption volatility persists within countries. Not only might poverty rates fluctuate from one year to another, but even if aggregate poverty rates are constant over time, the share of the population which is vulnerable to poverty, i.e. which is poor 'only' from time to time, might be much higher. Moreover, these poverty measures cannot assess whether high poverty rates are a cause of structural poverty (i.e. low endowments) or a cause of poverty risk (i.e. high uninsured income fluctuations), which is important to know from a policy perspective.

To overcome the shortcomings of traditional poverty assessments, which can only present a *static* picture of households' welfare, vulnerability measures estimate the *ex-ante* welfare of households, taking into account the *dynamic* dimension of poverty. Vulnerability assessments, therefore, try to estimate ex-ante both

[1]Here, and in the following, idiosyncratic shocks refer to household-specific shocks (e.g. injury, birth, death or job loss of a household member) that are either uncorrelated or only weakly correlated across households within a community. Covariate shocks refer to shocks that are correlated across households within communities but uncorrelated (or only weakly correlated) across communities, i.e. they can be defined as community-specific shocks (e.g. natural disasters or epidemics).

the expected mean as well as variance of consumption, with the latter being determined by idiosyncratic and covariate shocks.

Although there has recently been a growing theoretical literature on vulnerability measurement, relevant empirical studies on vulnerability are - largely due to data limitations - still rare. Apart from the fact that only past welfare data is and will always only be available to assess future welfare, vulnerability analysis is so far also severely constrained by missing data on the two most important dimensions of vulnerability.

First, to appropriately examine the *dynamic* aspects of poverty, lengthy panel data on income *and* consumption would be needed. But for many developing countries, lengthy panel data does not exist and cross-sectional surveys (or sometimes panels with two or three waves), with *either* income *or* consumption data, are the only data available. Second, to assess the underlying *causes* of vulnerability, comprehensive data on shocks and coping strategies would be necessary. However, most household surveys were not designed to provide a full accounting of the impact of shocks on households' income or consumption and information on idiosyncratic and covariate shocks is in most data sets either completely missing or very limited.

Most existing empirical studies have, therefore, either examined the vulnerability of households, ignoring the causes of the observed vulnerability, or have only studied the impact of selected idiosyncratic or covariate selected shocks on households' consumption, leaving out an analysis of the relative importance of different shocks on households' vulnerability. In addition, concentrating on selected shocks might have led to biased and inefficient estimates of the impact of these shocks on households' vulnerability (see Section 3.2.2).

The objective of this paper is to assess the relative impact of idiosyncratic and covariate shocks on households' vulnerability to poverty. More precisely, we both estimate how much of households' vulnerability is structural and risk induced and estimate the share of risk induced vulnerability that is idiosyncratic and covariate. We propose a simple method which can be applied to commonly available living standard household measurement surveys (LSMS) without being constrained by the usual data limitations for vulnerability analysis; i.e. the method allows to estimate the impact of idiosyncratic and covariate shocks on households' vulnerability without lengthy panel data and information on a wide range of shocks. The suggested approach is an integration of multilevel analysis (Goldstein 1999) into the widely applied method by Chaudhuri (2002) to estimate vulnerability from cross-sectional or short panel data to overcome the problem of missing lengthy panel data.

We are aware of the fact that rather strong assumptions have to be made to estimate households' vulnerability based on data from a single or only few points in time. However, given that lengthy panel data is missing for most developing countries, we argue that the suggested approach can provide quite interesting insights into the relative impact of idiosyncratic and covariate shocks on households' consumption fluctuations. The suggested approach should not serve as an alternative to the use of lengthy panel data, which are in any case preferable, but rather as an attempt to apply the concept of vulnerability to available cross-sectional or short panel data.

The remaining paper is structured as follows. Section 3.2 briefly discusses the theoretical and empirical literature on vulnerability to poverty. Section 3.3 proposes a methodology that allows assessing the relative importance of idiosyncratic and covariate shocks for households' vulnerability. Section 3.4 presents an empirical application to Madagascar and Section 3.5 concludes.

## 3.2 Concepts and Estimates of Vulnerability

As discussed in the introduction, a household's currently observed poverty status might not be a reliable guide to a household's longer-term wellbeing. Policy and research in development economics have, therefore, long emphasized that it is crucial to go beyond a static ex-post assessment of who is currently poor to a dynamic ex-ante assessment of who is vulnerable to poverty. But although there has been an emerging literature mainly on the concept but also on the empirical analysis of vulnerability, its significance is especially for policy makers still rather low. This will be discussed in the following two sections.

### 3.2.1 Concepts of Vulnerability

The current theoretical literature on vulnerability is still in a rather early stage of research with numerous definitions and measures and seemingly no consensus on how to conceptualize vulnerability (see also Hoddinott and Quisumbing, 2003). Several competing measures have been proposed (for an overview see e.g. Hoddinott and Quisumbing, 2003) but the literature has not yet settled on a preferred definition or measure. In principal, however, three main concepts of vulnerability have emerged:

Combining the literature on imperfect insurance with an assessment of prospective risks, the first approach proposes to measure vulnerability as uninsured exposure to risks, or in other words, the ability of households to insure consumption against income fluctuations (e.g. Glewwe and Hall, 1998). The second concept defines vulnerability as expected poverty, i.e. as the probability that a household's future consumption will lie below a pre-defined poverty line (e.g. Chaudhuri, 2002; Pritchett et al., 2000b). The third definition associates vulnerability with low expected utility (Ligon and Schechter, 2003). Based on micro-economic theory, that the utility of risk-averse individuals falls if volatility of consumption rises, vulnerability is measured with reference to the utility derived from some level of certain-equivalent-consumption, above which households would not be considered as vulnerable. Last, using an axiomatic approach, Calvo and Dercon (2005) have combined the latter two measures and define vulnerability as 1 minus the expected value of the ratio of a household's consumption to the poverty line with an exponent between 0 and 1 to account for risk aversion.[2]

But independent of the applied definition of vulnerability, vulnerability measures are always a function of the estimated expected mean and variance of households' consumption. The mean of expected consumption is determined by household and community characteristics whereas the variance in households' consumption is determined by the severity and frequency[3] of idiosyncratic and covariate shocks as well as the strength of households' coping mechanisms to insure consumption against these shocks.

For a comprehensive understanding of vulnerability to poverty it is also important to know both the magnitude of consumption volatility (i.e. the level of

[2]More precisely, the formula is $V = 1 - \sum_{i=1}^{I} p_i (\frac{x_i}{z})^{\alpha}$, where $p_i$ is the probability and $x_i$ the consumption of state $i$. $z$ is the poverty line and $\alpha$ a risk-aversion factor between 0 and 1. Whenever $x_i$ is greater than $z$, the ratio is set to 1.

[3]The question of the impact of the frequency of shocks on households consumption is often ignored, as lengthy data on the probability distribution of shocks is practical not available.

vulnerability) as well as the causes of volatility in consumption (i.e. the sources of vulnerability). In general, currently available data does, however, only barely allow to estimate the vulnerability of households or the impact of shocks on consumption, let alone to measure both the level and sources of vulnerability simultaneously. The existing empirical literature on vulnerability analysis can, therefore, be broadly divided into two strands of literature: the first concentrating on the measurement of aggregate vulnerability within a population and the latter analyzing the impact of selected shocks on households' consumption.

### 3.2.2 Estimates of Vulnerability

The first strand of literature, which intends to estimate the vulnerability of households, has been pioneered by Townsend (1994, 1995) and Udry (1995) who were some of the first using panel data to analyze whether households are able to insure consumption against *idiosyncratic* income fluctuations over space and time. In this spirit, several studies followed, 'simply' analyzing consumption fluctuations over time (e.g. Dercon and Krishnan, 2000; Jalan and Ravallion, 1999; Morduch, 2005).

A severe drawback of this literature is that it relies on panel data (and often also on the presence of *both* income *and* consumption data), which is very limited for developing countries. The existing studies and drawn conclusions are hence often based on very few rounds (often not more than 2 waves) and/or observations (often not more than 100 households) of rural panel data, whereas urban households are mostly ignored (Morduch, 2005). A major confounding factor is also the problem of measurement error as it is quite difficult to distinguish real consumption changes from measurement error in these relatively short panels (see e.g. Luttmer, 2000; Woolard and Klasen, 2005).

The second strand of empirical literature on vulnerability which estimates the impact of selected shocks on households' consumption has also large data-driven limitations. Information on idiosyncratic and covariate shocks is in most households surveys very limited and sometimes even completely missing. As a consequence, most authors have only focused on the impact of selected shocks on consumption (see e.g. Gertler and Gruber, 2002; Glewwe and Hall, 1998; Grimm, 2006; Kochar, 1995; Paxon, 1992; Woolard and Klasen, 2005).

Concentrating on certain shocks does, however, not allow for an analysis of the relative impact of various shocks on households' consumption, which would be needed to assess which shocks should be given first priority in 'poverty-prevention' programs. Moreover, these studies have rarely been able to analyze the impact of these shocks on the vulnerability of households, as households' vulnerability to shocks is not only a function of the impact of shocks on households' consumption but also of the frequency distribution of these shocks.

In addition, there are severe econometric problems related to this work. Most studies rely on standard regression analysis (ordinary least squares, OLS) to study the impact of shocks on households' consumption. First, focusing on certain shocks introduces a considerable omitted variable bias as various shocks are often highly correlated (see Table 3.1 for Madagascar). The impact of selected shocks on households' consumption is therefore likely to be overestimated. On the other hand, the impact of other shocks might be underestimated, if the impact of these shocks depends on the occurrence of other shocks, and hence would only be significant in an interaction term.

Table 3.1: Correlation of Selected Covariate Shocks

| | Malaria | Tuber | Typhoid | Cholera | Rice | Newcastle | Flood | Road | Drought |
|---|---|---|---|---|---|---|---|---|---|
| Malaria | 1.00 | | | | | | | | |
| Tuber* | 0.60 | 1.00 | | | | | | | |
| Typhoid | 0.40 | 0.44 | 1.00 | | | | | | |
| Cholera | 0.39 | 0.36 | 0.34 | 1.00 | | | | | |
| Rice* | 0.25 | 0.21 | 0.18 | 0.03 | 1.00 | | | | |
| Newcastle* | 0.63 | 0.49 | 0.29 | 0.34 | 0.15 | 1.00 | | | |
| Flood | 0.15 | 0.15 | 0.24 | 0.17 | 0.00 | 0.20 | 1.00 | | |
| Road* | 0.29 | 0.18 | 0.26 | 0.15 | 0.14 | 0.19 | 0.36 | 1.00 | |
| Drought | 0.26 | 0.24 | 0.28 | 0.06 | 0.20 | 0.18 | 0.09 | -0.02 | 1.00 |

*Source:* ILO/Cornell Commune Level census 2001. Computations by the authors.
*Notes:* *) Tuber: Tuberculosis. Rice: Rice Pest. Newcastle: Cattle Disease. Road: Impassible Road or Bridge.

Second, it is often assumed that the impact of shocks on consumption is the same across all households, which is a rather strong assumption to make. We should, for example, expect that the marginal effect of shocks on households' consumption is lower for households at the upper end of the income distribution as these households should posses better self-insurance mechanisms. Third, the problem of endogeneity might be severe as households' welfare has presumably also an impact on the occurrence of certain shocks. For example, poor households normally face higher mortality risks.

Most important, several studies, which have analyzed the impact of covariate community shocks might be biased because they disregard the hierarchical (or multilevel) data structure underlying these estimates (Goldstein, 1997, 1999).[4] If covariate community shocks are simply assigned to each household within a community, 'blowing up' data values from a small number of communities to many more households, the assumption of independent observations is violated, leading to estimates that might be statistically insignificant and hence overestimate the impact of covariate shocks on households' consumption (for a more detailed discussion see Section 3.3.1).

### 3.2.3 Idiosyncratic and Covariate Shocks

We certainly cannot bridge the data gaps that exist with regard to missing panel data and missing information on shocks in developing countries. What we propose is an estimation method which allows to study the relative impact of idiosyncratic and covariate shocks on households' vulnerability, without lengthy panel data and without facing the discussed econometric problems that usually occur when estimating the impact of certain selected shocks on households' consumption. In addition, we estimate the level and sources of vulnerability simultaneously, which has rarely been done. Although we cannot distinguish between the impact of specific shocks, a disaggregation of the impact of covariate community versus idiosyncratic household-specific shocks should already be interesting.

Since covariate (community) shocks are correlated across households, mutual insurance mechanisms within communities can easily break down during covariate 'crisis'. On the other hand, mutual insurance across communities, which

[4]We speak of hierarchical data structure or multilevel data whenever variables, i.e. economic indicators, are collected at different hierarchical levels with lower hierarchical levels, e.g. households, nested within higher hierarchical levels, e.g. communities (for a detailed discussion of multilevel data structure see Section 3.3.2).

would mitigate the problem of correlated shocks across households, are hypothesized to break down because of information asymmetries and enforcement limitations (Ray, 1998). On the contrary, micro-economic theory claims that households are (imperfectly) able to insure consumption against idiosyncratic shocks, as they are uncorrelated across households even within communities, where information asymmetries and enforcement limitations are assumed to be less severe than across communities. Hence, analyzing the relative magnitude of covariate and idiosyncratic variance in households' consumption can first of all test the hypothesis of better insurance mechanisms against idiosyncratic shocks than again covariate shocks.

In addition, an assessment of the relative importance of idiosyncratic and covariate shocks might help policy makers to set up insurance priorities. Possible insurance mechanisms for idiosyncratic on the one hand and covariate shocks on the other hand might differ quite significantly. Whereas higher information asymmetries persist for *mutual* or *informal* insurance mechanisms *across* communities, the contrary is the case for *external* or *formal* insurance mechanisms where higher information asymmetries prevail for shocks and consumption volatility *within* communities. Moreover, in contrast to idiosyncratic shocks, covariate shocks are much easier to target *externally*, as they are geographically clustered.

Few studies (e.g. Carter, 1997; Dercon and Krishnan, 2000) have attempted to estimate the relative importance of covariate and idiosyncratic shocks on households' consumption. Their estimation results generally show that covariate shocks have a larger and more significant impact on households' consumption than idiosyncratic shocks. However, these studies have often only analyzed rural households, relied on lengthy panel data, which is rarely available for developing countries, and also faced the discussed econometric problems of concentrating on some selected idiosyncratic and covariate shocks, without taking into account hierarchical data structure. Moreover, assessing the relative impact of idiosyncratic and covariate shocks based on a classification of shocks into covariate and idiosyncratic shocks is problematic as several shocks have an idiosyncratic and a covariate component.[5] Hence, we think that our approach, which will be discussed in the fol-

[5]For example, it is difficult to say whether the death of a household member is an idiosyncratic or a covariate shock, as the death might have occurred because of age - in this case the death were

lowing, might contribute to a better understanding of the relative importance of idiosyncratic and covariate shocks on households' vulnerability.

## 3.3 Methodology

### 3.3.1 Mean and Variance of Consumption

Our proposed method is an extension of the methodology proposed by Chaudhuri (2002) to estimate expected mean and variance in consumption using cross-sectional data or short panel data. This estimation procedure has recently become quite popular to analyze vulnerability, as lengthy panel data is practically not available for developing countries. In the following, we only present the estimation procedure for cross-sectional data although the same method can be applied to short panel data.[6]

The main hypothesis, that Chaudhuri (2002) makes to estimate the expected mean and variance of consumption, is that the error term in a consumption regression, or the unexplained variance in consumption of otherwise equal households, captures the impact of household-specific idiosyncratic and community-specific covariate shocks on households's consumption. Furthermore, the assumption is made that this variance is correlated, i.e. can be explained, with observable household and community characteristics.

Suppose that the consumption of household $i (i = 1, ..., n)$ in period $t$ is determined by a set of variables $X_i$.[7] We can hence write down the following equation:

$$\ln c_i = \beta_0 + \beta_1 X_i + e_i \tag{3.1}$$

an idiosyncratic shock - or because of an epidemic - in this case the death constituted a covariate shock.

[6]For a discussion of implementing the proposed method using panel data with a two-wave panel see Chaudhuri (2002) or Ligon and Schechter (2004). Chaudhuri (2002) uses a two-wave panel data set from Indonesia between 1998 and 1999. Ligon and Schechter (2004) use a two-wave panel from Vietnam (1993 and 1998) and Bulgaria (1994 and 1995).

[7]Note that the subscript $i$ in this section refers to the household *and* community subscripts $i$ and $j$ in Section 3.3.2. In Chaudhuri (2002) no explicit difference is made between household and community characteristics and shocks, i.e. error terms.

where $\ln c_i$ is per capita household (log) consumption, $X_i$ a set of household as well as community characteristics, and $e_i$ the unexplained part of households' consumption, i.e. the impact of shocks on households' consumption. As we assume that the impact of shocks on households' consumption is also correlated with observable household and community characteristics, we can define the variance of the unexplained part of households' consumption $e_i$ as:

$$\sigma_{ei}^2 = \theta_0 + \theta_1 X_i + \eta_i. \tag{3.2}$$

Hence, whereas standard ordinary least squares (OLS) regression techniques assume homoscedasticity, i.e. the same variance $V(e_i) = \sigma^2$ across all households, Chaudhuri (2002) assumes that the variance of the error term is not equal across households but depends on $X_i$, i.e. is heteroscedastic,[8] reflecting the impact of shocks on households' consumption. Since we assume heteroscedasticity, using OLS for an estimation of $\beta$ and $\theta$ would lead to unbiased but inefficient coefficients. To overcome this problem, equation 3.1 has to be reduced to a model where the residuals $e_i$ have a homogeneous variance.[9]

In a last step, for each household, the expected mean (equation 3.3) and variance (equation 3.4) of consumption can be estimated using consistent and asymptotically efficient estimators $\hat{\beta}$ and $\hat{\theta}$:

$$\hat{E}[\ln c_i|X] = \hat{\beta} X_i \tag{3.3}$$

$$\hat{V}[\ln c_i|X] = \hat{\sigma}_{ei}^2 = \hat{\theta} X_i. \tag{3.4}$$

We expand the proposed method by Chaudhuri (2002) with multilevel analysis (Goldstein, 1999). This first of all allows to differentiate between unexplained variance at the household level (i.e. the impact of idiosyncratic household-specific shocks) and unexplained variance at the community level (i.e. the impact of covariate community-specific shocks). Second, multilevel analysis corrects for inefficient estimators, which might occur whenever the proposed methodology by Chaudhuri (2002) is applied to hierarchical data structures, i.e. whenever household and community variables are used in equation (3.1) and (3.2) simultaneously.

[8]It is still assumed that the conditional distribution of $e_i$ has a mean of zero.

[9]For a detailed discussion, see Maddala (1977). Chaudhuri (2002), for example, applies three-step feasible generalized least squares.

### 3.3.2 Multilevel Analysis

Multilevel models are designed to analyze the relationship between variables that are measured at different hierarchical levels (for an introduction see e.g. Bryk and Raudenbush, 1992; Goldstein, 1999; Hox, 2002). We speak of 'hierarchical' or 'multilevel' data structure whenever variables are collected at different hierarchical *levels* with lower levels (e.g. households) nested within higher levels (e.g. communities).

Using a multilevel model first of all allows to use both individual observations and groups of observations simultaneously in the same model without violating the assumption of independent observations, providing correct standard errors and significance tests (Goldstein 1999). If this data structure were ignored, for example if a certain community characteristic were simply assigned to each household living within this community, the assumption of independent observations would be ignored, leading to downward biased standard errors and overestimated *t*-values. As a result the precision of estimates would be overstated.[10]

Moreover, multilevel models do not only account for dependencies between individual observations but also explicitly analyze dependencies at each level and across levels. In a multilevel model each level is formally represented by its own sub-model, which expresses not only the relationships among variables within the given level but also across different levels. For example, multilevel models would assume that covariate shocks do not only have a direct impact on households consumption,[11] but also an indirect impact on the returns to household-specific characteristics.[12]

[10]A related problem of dependent individual observations, leading to biased standard errors, also occurs in surveys with cluster sampling. Several methods have been proposed to estimate unbiased standard errors in clustered survey samples (Deaton, 1997) and in principle these correction procedures could also be applied to hierarchical data structure. However, and in contrast to multilevel models, most of the proposed procedures for cluster sampling assume intra-class correlations between observations within clusters that are equal for all variables, which is usually not the case for variables of different hierarchical levels (Hox, 2002).

[11]This direct impact is assumed to be the same for all households within the same community.

[12]In contrast, to control for sample clustering, usual regression techniques assume constant intra-class correlations for all variables, ignoring the relationship of variables at each level and between variables of different hierarchical levels.

Last, and most important for our case, multilevel models decompose the unexplained variance of the dependent variable (e.g. consumption) into a lower-level (e.g. household) and higher-level (e.g. community) component which we use for an assessment of the impact of idiosyncratic households-specific versus covariate community-specific shocks on households' consumption.

To formally illustrate the basic idea of multilevel modeling suppose $i = 1,...,I$ units (e.g. households) at level one and $j = 1,...,J$ units (e.g. communities) at level two and that household $i$ is nested within community $j$. If $\ln c_{ij}$ is per capita household (log) consumption and $X_{ij}$ a set of household characteristics of household $i$ in community $j$ we can set up the following regression equation:

$$\ln c_{ij} = \beta_{0j} + \beta_{1j} X_{ij} + e_{ij} \tag{3.5}$$

where the error term $e_{ij}$ reflects the unexplained variance in households' consumption. Note that in contrast to standard regression models and equation (3.1), the variables in equation (3.5) are denoted by two subscripts: one referring to the household $i$ and one to the community $j$, and that coefficients are denoted by a subscript referring to the community $j$. This means that it is assumed that $\beta_{0j}$ and $\beta_{1j}$ vary across communities. Various community characteristics $Z_j$ can then be introduced to estimate the variance of coefficients across communities:

$$\beta_{0j} = \gamma_{00} + \gamma_{01} Z_j + u_{0j} \tag{3.6}$$

$$\beta_{1j} = \gamma_{10} + \gamma_{11} Z_j + u_{1j}. \tag{3.7}$$

where the error terms $u_{0j}$ and $u_{1j}$ represent level two residuals, i.e. the unexplained variance in consumption across communities.[13] Equation (3.6) and (3.7) hence reflect the impact of community characteristics $Z_j$ on households' consumption, which differs across communities but which is the same for all households within the same community $j$. Substituting equation (3.6) and (3.7) into equation (3.5) provides the full model, which can be written as

$$\ln c_{ij} = \overbrace{\gamma_{00} + \gamma_{01} Z_j + (\gamma_{10} + \gamma_{11} Z_j) X_{ij}}^{deterministic} + \overbrace{u_{0j} + u_{1j} X_{ij} + e_{ij}}^{stochastic}. \tag{3.8}$$

[13]The residuals $e_{ij}$, $u_{0j}$ and $u_{1j}$ are assumed to have a mean of zero.

and estimated via maximum likelihood (Mason et al., 1983; Goldstein, 1999; Bryk and Raudenbush, 1992). The first part of equation (3.8) reflects the deterministic part of the equation, including the interaction term $X_{ij}Z_j$, which analyzes cross-level interactions between variables at the household and variables at the community level. The second part captures the stochastic part of the model.

In contrast to standard OLS regression the error term in (3.8) contains not only an individual or household component $e_{ij}$ but also a group or community component $u_{0j} + u_{1j}X_{ij}$. The error term $u_{0j}$ represents the unexplained variance across communities for the intercept $\beta_{0j}$. The error term $u_{1j}$ reflects the unexplained variance across communities for the slope $\beta_{1j}$. The error term $e_{ij}$ captures the remaining unexplained variance in households' consumption.

This is nicely illustrated in Figure 3.1, where the error terms $u_0$, $u_1$, and $e_i$ are illustrated for community $j$.[14] The lower solid line represents the intercept and slope that can be estimated with the specific community characteristics $Z_j$ of community $j$ with equation (3.6) and (3.7). The upper solid line indicates the 'predicted' intercept $\beta_{0j}$ and slope $\beta_{1j}$ within community $j$ estimated with the household characteristics $X_{ij}$ in equation (3.5). Thus if we consider any household observation $i$, the unexplained part of consumption $\ln c_i$, can be decomposed into $u_0$ (referring to the unexplained part of the community-specific intercept), $u_1$ (referring to the unexplained part of the community-specific slope), and $e_i$ (referring to the household-specific error term).

The stochastic part in equation (3.8) also demonstrates the problem of dependent errors in multilevel analysis. Whereas the household error component $e_{ij}$ is independent across all households, the community level errors $u_{0j}$ and $u_{1j}$ are independent between communities but dependent, i.e. equal, for every household $i$ within community $j$. This already leads to heteroscedastic error terms, as the overall error term of a household depends on $u_{0j}$ and $u_{1j}$ as well as on household characteristics $X_{ij}$. For the case that the household- and community-specific error terms $e_{ij}$, $u_{1j}$, and $u_{0j}$ are themselves heteroscedastic - an assumption we make

[14] Note that intercepts and slopes vary across communities $j = 1, \ldots J$ but not across households $i = 1, \ldots I$ within a community $j$.

Figure 3.1: Error Terms of Multilevel Modeling

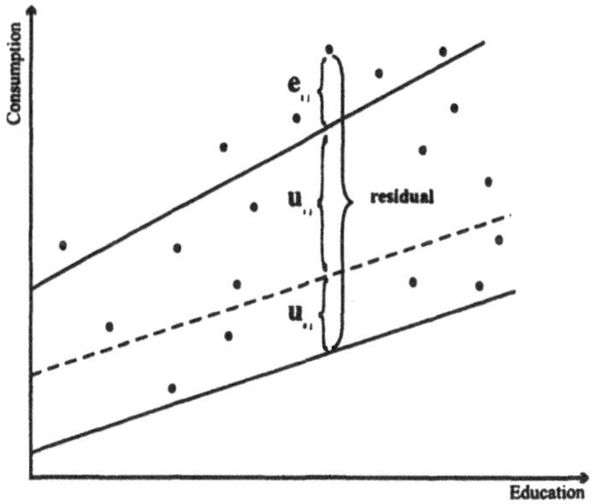


*Source:* Own Illustration.
*Notes:* $u_{0j}$: Community-specific error term of the community-specific intercept $\beta_{0j}$, see equation (3.6). $u_{1j}$: Community-specific error term of the community-specific slope $\beta_{1j}$, see equation (3.7). $e_{ij}$: Household-specific error term in community $j$.

- multilevel modeling also allows to specify heteroscedasticity at the community and household level.[15]

### 3.3.3 Idiosyncratic and Covariate Variance

To assess the relative impact of idiosyncratic and covariate shocks on households' vulnerability using cross-sectional data we incorporate multilevel modeling (described in Section 3.3.2) into the method of Chaudhuri (2002) (described in Section 3.3.1).

In a first step, using a basic multilevel model, we regress per capita household (log) consumption of household $i$ in community $j$ on a set of household $X_{ij}$ and community covariates $Z_j$, which can be denoted:

$$\ln c_{ij} = \gamma_{00} + \gamma_{10} X_{ij} + \gamma_{01} Z_j + (u_j + e_{ij}). \tag{3.9}$$

[15] For the estimation of the multilevel model, the GLAMM package for STATA is used. To provide consistent and asymptotically efficient estimators, the Huber/White sandwich estimator is used (see e.g. Maas and Hox, 2004).

Note that in contrast to equation (3.8) no cross-level interactions are included in equation (3.9), i.e. the interaction term $\gamma_{10}Z_jX_{ij}$ and the error term $u_{1j}X_{ij}$ are set to zero. When setting up the multilevel model, we also included cross-level interaction terms, which did however not show any significant results. Since interaction terms should only be incorporated in multilevel models if they show significant results (see e.g. Hox, 2002), they were removed from the model. This means that community characteristics and shocks only have a direct impact on households' consumption and no impact on the returns to household characteristics. Whether this holds for other data sets is a further interesting research question.

Equation (3.9) hence estimates two error terms, one at the household level $e_{ij}$ and one at the community level $u_j$. Following Chaudhuri (2002) it is assumed that the error term $e_{ij}$ at the household level captures the impact of idiosyncratic shocks whereas the error term $u_j$ at the community level captures the impact of covariate shocks on households' consumption. Again following Chaudhuri (2002), we assume that the variance of consumption at the household and at the community level, i.e. the impact of idiosyncratic and covariate shocks, depends on a set of household and community characteristics:

$$\sigma^2_{e_{ij}} = \theta_0 + \theta_1 X_{ij} + \theta_2 Z_j \tag{3.10}$$

$$\sigma^2_{u_j} = \tau_0 + \tau_1 Z_j \tag{3.11}$$

where $\sigma^2_{e_{ij}}$ refers to the variance at the household level (level 1) and $\sigma^2_{u_j}$ to the variance at the community level (level 2). In a second step, we can therefore estimate the variance at the household level $\sigma^2_{eij}$ and the community level $\sigma^2_{uj}$ from the predicted residuals $e_{ij}$ and $u_j$ of equation (3.9) using again a multilevel approach that provides us with asymptotically efficient and consistent estimation parameters for each variance component.[16]

In a third step, we finally estimate the expected mean as well as the idiosyncratic and covariate variance of households' consumption:

$$\hat{E}[\ln c_{ij}|X,Z] = \hat{\gamma}_{00} + \hat{\gamma}_{10}X_{ij} + \hat{\gamma}_{01}Z_j \tag{3.12}$$

[16] In this model estimates of $\sigma^2_{e_{ij}}$ and $\sigma^2_{u_j}$ do not necessarily have to be positive. We did not face this problem in our case. However, an alternative way to estimate the variance of consumption, which guarantees positive values, is to use the log of variance in consumption so that equation (3.10) and equation (3.11) become $\log(\sigma^2_{e_{ij}}) = \theta_0 + \theta_1 X_{ij} + \theta_2 Z_j$ and $\log(\sigma^2_{u_j}) = \tau_0 + \tau_1 Z_j$.

$$\hat{V}_{idiosyncratic}[\ln c_i|X,Z] = \hat{\sigma}^2_{e_{ij}} = \hat{\theta}_0 + \hat{\theta}_1 X_{ij} + \hat{\theta}_2 Z_j \quad (3.13)$$

$$\hat{V}_{covariate}[\ln c_i|Z] = \hat{\sigma}^2_{u_j} = \hat{\tau}_0 + \hat{\tau}_1 Z_j. \quad (3.14)$$

These estimates can be used to asses the impact of idiosyncratic and covariate shocks on households' vulnerability, applying any of the measures of vulnerability (see Section 3.2.1).

### 3.3.4 Critical Discussion

Obviously, in the absence of any time-variant information on consumption, three rather strong assumptions have to be made when using cross-sectional surveys to estimate expected mean and variance in consumption.

First, the most critical assumption is that it has to be assumed that present cross-sectional variance can be used to estimate future inter-temporal variance in consumption. This implicitly assumes that the variance in consumption of a particular household is constant over time, i.e. that $Var(e_{it}) = \sigma_i^2$. Moreover, although cross-sectional variance might explain part of inter-temporal variance due to idiosyncratic or covariate community-specific shocks, the model will always miss the impact of inter-temporal shocks on the national level.

The argument for justifying this assumption is the non-existence of panel data in developing countries, but one should be aware of the limitations of a conclusion about inter-temporal variance in consumption that is based on estimates from a single period. Also for short panel data, this assumption remains very critical. Only lengthy panel data would allow to draw precise conclusions about inter-temporal variance in consumption, since it includes information on changes in consumption over time. On the other hand, one could argue that panel estimators use *past* variance to estimate *future* variance in consumption, which might not always be better.

Second, it has to be assumed that the impact of shocks on households' consumption is indeed correlated with observable characteristics. In addition, the above model also assumes that shocks have no impact on the covariates $X_{ij}$ or $Z_j$, which might not hold in all cases. For example, a death in a household would also have an effect on the household size, captured by $X_{ij}$.

Last, the existence of measurement error and unobserved heterogeneity in households' characteristics, which determine households' consumption, is a major concern for the estimation of variance in consumption. Large measurement error and unobserved but deterministic heterogeneity in households' characteristics could lead to a significant overestimation of the variance in consumption, i.e. a general overestimation of the impact of idiosyncratic and covariate shocks on households' consumption.

Hence, it has to be assumed that the error term in equation (3.1) mainly captures some 'economic' variance and only to a lesser extent measurement error in consumption.[17] This assumption is however not only made in other (panel) estimations of inter-temporal consumption variance (see e.g. Townsend, 1994) but also in other strands of literature (e.g. the error term in wage equations capturing unmeasured skill diversity, see Lemieux, 2006). With regard to high unobserved but deterministic heterogeneity in households' characteristics, there is little we can do. Thus, whenever we assume high unobserved deterministic heterogeneity, short panel data should be preferred to cross-sectional data - using the same methodology of Chaudhuri (2002) - to control for household-specific fixed effects.

The proposed method has, however, the great advantage that it overcomes the problem of missing lengthy panel data. In addition, Chaudhuri (2003) demonstrates the robustness of the above described approach using a two-year panel of Indonesia and the Philippines, comparing estimated *ex-ante* poverty rates from the vulnerability estimates in the first year with the actual incidence of poverty in the second year.[18]

Furthermore, conducting Monte Carlo experiments Ligon and Schechter (2004) show that the proposed approach of Chaudhuri (2002) is the 'best' so far proposed estimator of households' mean and variance in consumption whenever expenditure is measured with low error and whenever at least a *two-wave* panel is at

[17] Note that measurement error is also a major problem in estimators of vulnerability which are based on panel data.

[18] In the first round, given the estimated expected mean and variance in consumption of households, households were grouped based on their estimated probability to fall below the poverty line (see Section 3.4.3). The predicted poverty rates - which must be equal to the estimated mean probability to fall below the poverty line - for each decile of this poverty risk (or vulnerability) distribution matched almost exactly the actual poverty rates in the second round.

hand.[19] In any case, the proposed extension of Chaudhuri (2002) in Sections 3.3.2 and 3.3.3 can also easily be applied to short panel-data.

Keeping the critical assumptions in mind, the proposed approach should be understood as an illustrative attempt of assessing the vulnerability of households, when - as in most cases for developing countries - only cross-sectional or short panel data is at hand. As already discussed, there is no doubt that lengthy panel data are in any case preferable for the estimation of households' vulnerability. However, the extension of the concept of Chaudhuri (2002) with multilevel modeling might give interesting insights in the relative impact of idiosyncratic and covariate shocks on households' vulnerability whenever only cross-sectional data without any information about shocks is available.

## 3.4 Empirical Application

### 3.4.1 Data Description

We empirically illustrate our proposed approach for Madagascar. Madagascar is one of the poorest countries in sub-Saharan Africa with a GDP per capita of 744 US$ PPP and - according to the international poverty line of 1 US$ PPP a day - an estimated headcount poverty rate of 61.0 percent. Its poor economic performance is also reflected in very low indicators of human wellbeing: Life expectancy at birth is 55.6 years, under-five mortality rate is 123 in 1000, and child undernutrition (measured in weight for age for children below the age of 5) amounts up to 41.9 percent (UNDP, 2005). In addition, households in Madagascar are frequently hit by idiosyncratic and covariate shocks (Table 3.2) which have an additional severe down-side impact on households' wellbeing. Mills et al. (2003) further report that households are most often hit by frequently occurring covariate

[19] Ligon and Schechter (2004) do not recommend to estimate the mean and variance of households' consumption from one single cross-sectional data set, as a cross-sectional estimator only considers the part of consumption which can be predicted by observed characteristics as the base level of consumption. Ligon and Schechter (2004) argue that a large portion of consumption might however not be predicted by observed characteristics. Thus, as already discussed, we also have to assume low unobservable household-specific effects.

shocks, which also show a quite strong spatial and temporal correlation (see Table 3.1 and Table 3.2).

Table 3.2: Households' Exposure to Selected Shocks

| | Households in Communities with Exposure (in %) | Correlation of Shocks across Years (1999/2000)* |
|---|---|---|
| Epidemics | | |
| Malaria | 73.93 | 0.88 |
| Tuberculosis | 54.19 | 0.81 |
| Typhoid | 32.53 | 0.81 |
| Cholera | 33.64 | 0.44 |
| Agricultural shocks | | |
| Rice pest | 22.72 | 0.84 |
| Swineflu | 39.46 | 0.63 |
| Newcastle | 75.91 | 0.85 |
| Climate shocks | | |
| Flooding | 24.69 | 0.52 |
| Impassible bridge or road | 21.00 | 0.70 |
| Drought | 17.97 | 0.57 |
| Cyclones | 7.37 | 0.25 |

*Source: Enquete Auprès Des Menages*, 2001 and ILO/Cornell Commune Levels Census, 2001. Own calculations. *Mills et al., 2003.

The data, which we use for our analysis, is derived from a cross-sectional household survey and a cross-sectional community census. The community census is the 2001 ILO/Cornell Commune Level census, which provides information on community characteristics like social and economic infrastructure as well as data on the occurrence of covariate shocks. It covers 1,385 out of the 1,395 communities in Madagascar. Note that in many studies the village has been used as the 'natural' covariate level, but there is no necessity to do so (Genicot and Ray, 2003; Morduch, 2005), and using communities instead, as we do in this analysis, does not seem less useful. Data on household characteristics is taken from the national representative household survey of 2001 (*Enquete Auprès Des Menages*), covering 5,080 households (1,778 urban and 3,302 rural households) in 186 communities.

To estimate households' expected mean and variance of consumption, at the household level we use the stated household characteristics in Table 3.3. In ad-

Table 3.3: Summary Statistics for Households and Communities

| | Urban | Rural | National |
|---|---|---|---|
| Household demographic characteristics | | | |
| Age of HH head | 42.60 | 41.71 | 42.25 |
| Number of children | 1.70 | 2.16 | 1.88 |
| Female headed household (%) | 23.30 | 21.93 | 22.40 |
| Household Size | 4.42 | 4.78 | 4.56 |
| Household socioeconomic characteristics | | | |
| Residence (%) | 35.00 | 65.00 | 100.00 |
| Years of schooling of HH head | 7.80 | 4.15 | 6.35 |
| Works in agriculture (HH head) (%) | 41.02 | 83.00 | 57.68 |
| Works in informal sector (HH head) (%) | 22.88 | 7.04 | 16.59 |
| Works in formal sector (HH head) (%) | 21.74 | 5.80 | 15.41 |
| Works in public sector (HH head) (%) | 14.36 | 4.16 | 10.23 |
| Enterprize owner (%) | 30.22 | 20.24 | 26.26 |
| Land owner (%) | 31.51 | 86.82 | 53.40 |
| Number of cattle | 0.93 | 4.88 | 2.50 |
| Number of chicken | 2.63 | 8.70 | 5.04 |
| Community characteristics | | | |
| Telephone (%) | 83.16 | 18.75 | 57.60 |
| Sanitation (%) | 75.26 | 20.54 | 53.54 |
| Save water (%) | 98.43 | 50.00 | 79.21 |
| Electricity (%) | 98.43 | 42.00 | 76.02 |
| Hospital (%) | 93.01 | 7.14 | 58.53 |
| National road* (%) | 93.67 | 53.75 | 77.65 |
| Primary education (%) | 100 | 100 | 100 |
| Secondary education (%) | 100 | 67.86 | 87.16 |
| Tertiary education (%) | 97.89 | 10.71 | 63.07 |

*Source:* Community characteristics: ILO/Cornell Commune Level census 2001. Household characteristics: *Enquete Auprès Des Menages*, 2001. Computations by the authors.
*Notes:* *Unfortunately we do not have any information on graveled or paved roads.

dition, we consider an agricultural asset index (composed of seven productive assets) estimated via principal component analysis (Filmer and Pritchett, 2001). At the community level we include population density, mean educational level and percentage of households working in the formal sector and/or possesing an enterprise within the community. Moreover, we construct an infrastructure index, again based on principal component analysis, using several variables reflecting the infrastructure of the community (see Table 3.3).

Using an aggregate index for agricultural assets and community infrastructure instead of individual variables has two main reasons. First, the two chosen indices provide a proxy of the overall agricultural productivity of households and of the infrastructure within communities. Second, as households' (communities') endowment with different agricultural equipments (with different infrastructure facilities) is highly correlated, the coefficients of individual agricultural equipments (infrastructure facilities) would often not show any significant effects if they were included separately into regressions.

### 3.4.2 Estimation Results

As described in Section 3.3, we estimate the expected mean and variance per capita household (log) consumption using multilevel modeling. Moreover, we decompose the unexplained consumption variance into an idiosyncratic (household-level) and a covariate (community-level) component.

The regression results of the multilevel model for the estimated mean of (log) consumption are presented in Table 3.4. All coefficients show the expected signs, which are, however, not of interest for this study. The variance in consumption that is explained at each level is shown by $R_1^2$ and $R_2^2$, where $R_1^2$=0.38 refers to the explained variance at the household level within communities and $R_2^2$=0.66 refers to the explained variance at the community level. The $R^2$s did not improve when additional household and community characteristics were added.

We then applied a White-test to verify that the variance of both the error term $e_{ij}$ and $u_j$ is indeed heteroscedastic.[20] Last, we regressed the squared error terms, $(e_{ij}+u_j)^2$, $e_{ij}^2$, and $u_j^2$ on several household and community characteristics to estimate the total, idiosyncratic, and covariate variance in consumption for each household in our sample. Again we use a multilevel model.

The estimated average mean and variance in consumption for the whole sample are presented in Table 3.5, also separately for rural and urban households,

[20]The White-test regresses the squared residuals $u_i$ (in our case $e_{ij}$ and $u_j$) from a regression model $Y_i = \beta_0 + \beta_1 X_{1i} + \beta_2 X_{2i} + \ldots + \beta_n X_{ni} + u_i$ on the regressors $X_1, X_2 \ldots X_n$ (in our case $Xij$ and $Z_j$), as well as on the squares and the cross-products of the regressors to allow for non-linearities. An $F$-statistic is used to test the joint null hypothesis of all coefficients of the equation $u_i^2 = \delta_0 + \delta_1 X_{1i} + \delta_2 X_{2i} + \ldots + \delta_n X_{ni} + v_i$ being equal to zero: $H_0 = \hat{\delta}_1 = \hat{\delta}_2 = \ldots = \hat{\delta}_n = 0$. If $H_0$ is rejected, the error term $u_i$ is heteroscedastic.

Table 3.4: Regression Results for per capita (log) Consumption

| | Coeff. | Std. Error |
|---|---|---|
| Household demographic characteristics | | |
| Age of HH head** | 0.007 | 0.003 |
| $Age^2/100$ of HH head | 0.000 | 0.000 |
| Number of children** | -0.073 | 0.016 |
| Female headed household | 0.008 | 0.024 |
| Household Size** | -0.087 | 0.008 |
| Household socioeconomic characteristics | | |
| Years of schooling of HH head** | 0.053 | 0.001 |
| Works in agriculture (HH head) | ref. | |
| Works in informal sector (HH head)* | 0.081 | 0.032 |
| Works in formal sector (HH head)** | 0.119 | 0.026 |
| Works in public sector (HH head)** | 0.205 | 0.051 |
| Enterprize owner * | 0.041 | 0.024 |
| Land owner | 0.006 | 0.008 |
| Number of cattle** | 0.004 | 0.001 |
| Number of chicken | 0.001 | 0.001 |
| Agricultural asset index* | 0.024 | 0.012 |
| Community characteristics | | |
| Infrastructure index* | 0.035 | 0.020 |
| Population density* | 0.002 | 0.001 |
| Mean years of schooling** | 0.049 | 0.014 |
| % Working in formal sector** | 0.616 | 0.227 |
| % Enterprize owner** | 0.313 | 0.113 |
| $R_1^2$ | 0.376 | |
| $R_2^2$ | 0.664 | |
| Obs. level 1 (household) | 4694 | |
| Obs. level 2 (community) | 180 | |

*Source:* Community characteristics: ILO/Cornell Commune Level census 2001. Household characteristics: *Enquete Auprès Des Menages*, 2001. Computations by the authors.
*Notes:* * denotes significance at 10 % level and ** significance at 1 % level. $R_1^2$ refers to the explained variance at the household level and $R_2^2$ to the explained variance at the community level.

representing 65 percent and 35 percent of national households respectively. The expected per capita (log) consumption of rural households is considerably below the (log) poverty line, whereas the expected per capita (log) consumption of urban households lies considerably above the poverty line. This already suggests that low mean consumption is the main cause for rural vulnerability, whereas consumption volatility might be *relatively* more important for urban households.

Table 3.5: Mean and Standard Deviation of per capita (log) Consumption

| | Urban | Rural | National |
|---|---|---|---|
| Poverty line | 13.81 | 13.81 | 13.81 |
| Mean (estimated) | 14.38 | 13.54 | 13.80 |
| Standard Deviation (estimated) | | | |
| Total | 0.51 | 0.58 | 0.56 |
| Idiosyncratic | 0.53 | 0.47 | 0.49 |
| Covariate | 0.25 | 0.31 | 0.31 |
| Idiosyncratic / Covariate | 2.12 | 1.52 | 1.59 |

*Source:* ILO/Cornell Commune Level census 2001. *Enquete Auprès Des Menages*, 2001. Computations by the authors.
*Notes:* Estimates are household weighted and refer to per capita log consumption, adjusted for regional price differences.

With regard to the estimated variance in consumption, we show that the estimated variance is slightly higher for rural households than for urban households, with a standard deviation of 0.58 compared to 0.51 (Table 3.5). Interesting is that idiosyncratic variance is higher than covariate variance both for urban and rural households. However, the relative importance of idiosyncratic variance is higher for urban than for rural households. More precisely, whereas among urban households idiosyncratic standard deviation of consumption is 2.12 times as high as covariate standard deviation, the respective rate is only 1.52 for rural households.[21]

In this section, we analyzed the expected mean and variance of households' consumption separately but aggregated over all households. To obtain a full assessment of the level and sources of vulnerability, we have, however, to assess expected mean and variance of households' consumption jointly but separately for each household, which will be done in next section.

[21] Recall that we assumed, that the estimated variance in consumption on the household level reflects the impact of idiosyncratic shocks on household consumption whereas the estimated variance in consumption on the community level reflects the impact of covariate shocks on households' consumption.

### 3.4.3 Vulnerability to Poverty

Although all possible vulnerability definitions (or measurements) could be applied to analyze households' vulnerability with the estimated mean and variance in consumption of the previous section, we opt for the measurement proposed by Chaudhuri et al. (2002), defining vulnerability as the probability of a household to fall below the poverty line in the near future. The focus of this paper clearly lies on the estimation of vulnerability parameters (i.e. the mean and variance in consumption), so the applied measure of vulnerability only serves for illustrative purposes. Hence, we chose a measure that has in contrast to most other vulnerability measures an intuitive interpretation, although it might have some undesirable axiomatic properties (see Calvo and Dercon, 2005).

Assuming that consumption is log-normally distributed, we can estimate the probability of a household $i$ in community $j$ to fall below the poverty line using the estimated expected mean and variance of consumption:

$$\hat{\upsilon}_{ij} = \hat{P}_h(\ln c_{ij} < \ln z | X, Z) = \Phi\left(\frac{\ln z - \ln \hat{c}_{ij}}{\sqrt{\hat{\sigma}^2_{ij}}}\right) \tag{3.15}$$

where $\Phi(.)$ denotes the cumulative density of the standard normal distribution function, $z$ the poverty line, $\ln \hat{c}_{ij}$ the expected mean of per capita (log) consumption and $\hat{\sigma}^2_{ij}$ the estimated variance of per capita (log) consumption. The probability to fall below the poverty line is conducted separately for the estimated idiosyncratic variance $\sigma^2_{eij}$ and covariate variance $\sigma^2_{uj}$ in consumption as well as jointly $\sigma^2_{eij+uj}$ for the overall variance in consumption.

Last, we have to define a vulnerability threshold $\upsilon$ above which we consider households as vulnerable to poverty as well as a time horizon which we consider as the 'near' future. In the empirical literature often a vulnerability threshold of 50 percent and a time horizon of $t+2$ years is used (see e.g. Chaudhuri et al., 2002; Tesliuc and Lindert, 2004). This means, that those households are considered as vulnerable which have a 50 percent or higher probability to fall below the poverty line (at least once) in the next two years, $\upsilon_{ij,t+2} \geq 0.5$, which is equivalent to a 29 percent or higher probability $P$ to fall below the poverty line in any given year. Formally this can be derived from:

$$v_{ij,t+k} = 1 - [P(\ln c_{ij} > \ln z)]^k \tag{3.16}$$

where $v_{t+k}$ is the vulnerability threshold in $t$ to fall below the poverty line (at least once) in the next $k$ years. $P(\ln c_{ij} > \ln z)$ is the probability to have a consumption *above* the poverty line.

However, taking into account the critical assumptions that have to be made to draw conclusions about future variance in consumption with only cross-sectional data at hand, we constrain our analysis to a time horizon of $t+1$ with a vulnerability threshold of 25 percent. Certainly, any vulnerability threshold could be used, and the choice of a threshold of 25 percent is somewhat arbitrary but our focus is not on an absolute assessment of vulnerability but rather on the relative impact of idiosyncratic and covariate shocks on households' vulnerability. Furthermore, we check the robustness of our results to other vulnerability thresholds (see Figure 3.3).

Utilizing the stated vulnerability threshold and time horizon we estimate that 75 percent of households in Madagascar are vulnerable to poverty, i.e. 75 percent of households have a 25 percent or higher probability to fall below the poverty line in the next year (see also Table 3.6). The figures for urban and rural households are 43 and 89 percent respectively, indicating that rural households are much more vulnerable to poverty than urban households. Besides the vulnerability *rate*, we also calculate the *mean* vulnerability, or in other words the average probability to fall below the poverty line.[22] The estimated average probability to fall below the poverty line should approximately be equal to the observed poverty rate, i.e. the actual number of households which have fallen below the poverty line in the given year $t$, and can therefore serve to test whether the estimated mean vulnerability across all households is feasible (Chaudhuri et al., 2002). Both figures match to a very large extent (see also Table 3.6).

### 3.4.4 Sources of Vulnerability

Last, we decompose vulnerability estimates into sources of vulnerability. We first analyze whether vulnerability is mainly driven by permanent low consumption

[22] Note that the estimated mean vulnerability is in contrast to the vulnerability rate independent of any vulnerability threshold and/or time-horizon.

Figure 3.2: Poverty and Risk Induced Vulnerability

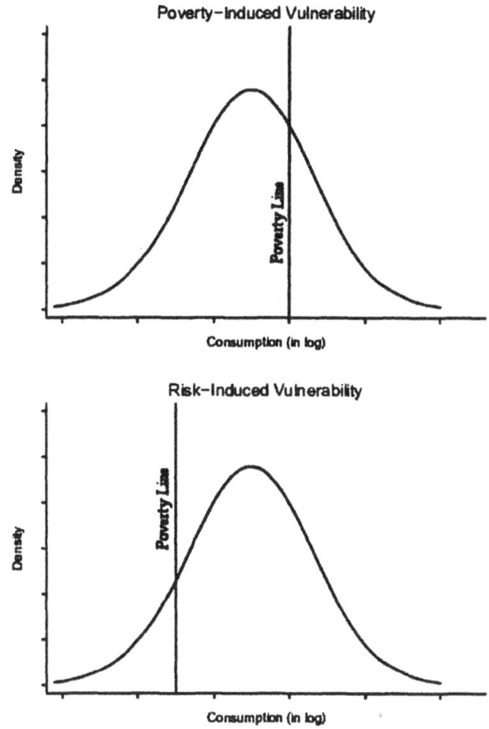


*Source:* Own illustration.

prospects (i.e. structural or poverty induced vulnerability) or by high consumption volatility (i.e. transitory or risk induced vulnerability).[23] In other words, if the (estimated) expected consumption $\ln \hat{c}_{ij}$ of a household $i$ in community $j$ already lies below the poverty line $\ln z$, then the household is referred to as structural or poverty-induced vulnerable (Figure 3.2). If the (estimated) expected consumption

[23] We implicitly assume that low expected mean consumption only reflects structural poverty and is not risk induced, although this does not necessarily have to be the case. Low consumption prospects can also be risk-induced through behavioral responses of households, e.g. engaging in low risk but also low return activities (Morduch, 1994; Elbers et al., 2003).

$\ln \hat{c}_{ij}$ lies above the poverty line $\ln z$, but a high estimated variance in consumption $\hat{\sigma}_{ij}^2$ still leads to an estimated vulnerability $\hat{v}_{ij,t+1} \geq 0.25$, then the household is said to face risk-induced or transitory vulnerability (Figure 3.2).

We see that rural vulnerability is mainly a cause of low expected mean in consumption whereas urban vulnerability is mainly driven by high consumption volatility (Table 3.6). More precisely, 66 percent of rural households have an expected per capita consumption that already lies below the poverty line, and 'only' 23 percent of rural households are vulnerable because of high consumption volatility. In contrast, only 11 percent of urban households face structural induced vulnerability whereas 33 percent face risk induced vulnerability (i.e. high consumption fluctuations). Even in absolute terms are urban households more vulnerable to consumption fluctuations (33 percent) than rural households (23 percent).

Table 3.6: Vulnerability Decomposition

| | Urban | Rural | National |
|---|---|---|---|
| Poverty Rate | 0.21 | 0.64 | 0.49 |
| Mean Vulnerability | 0.26 | 0.64 | 0.49 |
| Vulnerability Rate | 0.43 | 0.89 | 0.75 |
| Poverty Induced Vulnerability | 0.11 | 0.66 | 0.47 |
| Risk Induced Vulnerability | 0.33 | 0.23 | 0.28 |
| Poverty Induced / Risk Induced | 0.33 | 2.87 | 1.69 |
| Idiosyncratic Vulnerability | 0.38 | 0.85 | 0.71 |
| Covariate Vulnerability | 0.24 | 0.78 | 0.61 |
| Idiosyncratic / Covariate | 1.58 | 1.09 | 1.16 |

*Source:* ILO/Cornell Commune Level census 2001. *Enquete Auprès Des Menages*, 2001. Computations by the authors.
*Notes:* Estimates are household weighted. National Poverty Line: 990404 Madagascar Franc.

We further analyze the impact of idiosyncratic and covariate shocks on vulnerability to poverty. Table 3.6 shows, that idiosyncratic shocks have a slightly higher influence than covariate shocks on consumption volatility among rural households and a much higher influence than covariate shocks on households' consumption volatility in urban areas. 85 percent of rural and 38 percent of urban households are vulnerable to idiosyncratic shocks whereas 'only' 78 percent of rural and 24 percent of urban households are vulnerable to covariate shocks.

Note that in Section 3.3.1 we stated that in Chaudhuri's approach (2002) measurement error and unobserved but deterministic components of consumption might lead to an overall overestimation of the variance in households' consumption. Thus a higher vulnerability to idiosyncratic shocks could be caused by higher measurement error or higher unobserved heterogeneity of households at the individual level. However, even if that were the case, we could still assess the relative importance of idiosyncratic and covariate shocks for rural and urban households, with idiosyncratic shocks having a relatively higher impact on urban households' vulnerability and with covariate shocks having a relatively higher impact on rural households' consumption.

We check the robustness of our results to the chosen vulnerability threshold above which we consider households as being vulnerable to poverty in Figure 3.3. We show the percentage of households that have a probability between 0 and 1 or higher to fall below the poverty line (keeping the poverty line of ln 990,404 Madagascar Franc constant). At a threshold of 0, i.e. at a probability of 0 or higher to fall below the poverty line in the near future, every household is vulnerable to poverty, while at a threshold of 1, i.e. at a propability of 1 or higher to fall below the poverty line, no household is vulnerable to poverty. Estimates are provided for the whole population as well as separately for urban and rural households.

We marked the vulnerability threshold of 25 percent, which we used for our vulnerability analysis, providing us with the same estimates as presented in Table 3.6. As expected, the overall level of vulnerability increases with lower vulnerbility thresholds chosen and decreases with higher vulnerability thresholds. However, irrespective of the probability threshold, vulnerability to poverty is always higher in rural than in urban areas. Moreover, independent of the vulnerability threshold, covariate shocks are comparatively always more important for rural households than for urban households, whereas idiosyncratic shocks have a comparatively higher impact on urban households.[24]

[24]We also check the robustness of our results to all poverty lines across the entire income distribution (not shown here). For all poverty lines we obtain the same idiosyncratic and covariate vulnerability trends (for rural and urban households) as with a poverty line of ln 990,404 Madagascar Franc, but, as expected, on different levels.

## Figure 3.3: Cumulative Densities of Vulnerability - Probability Thresholds

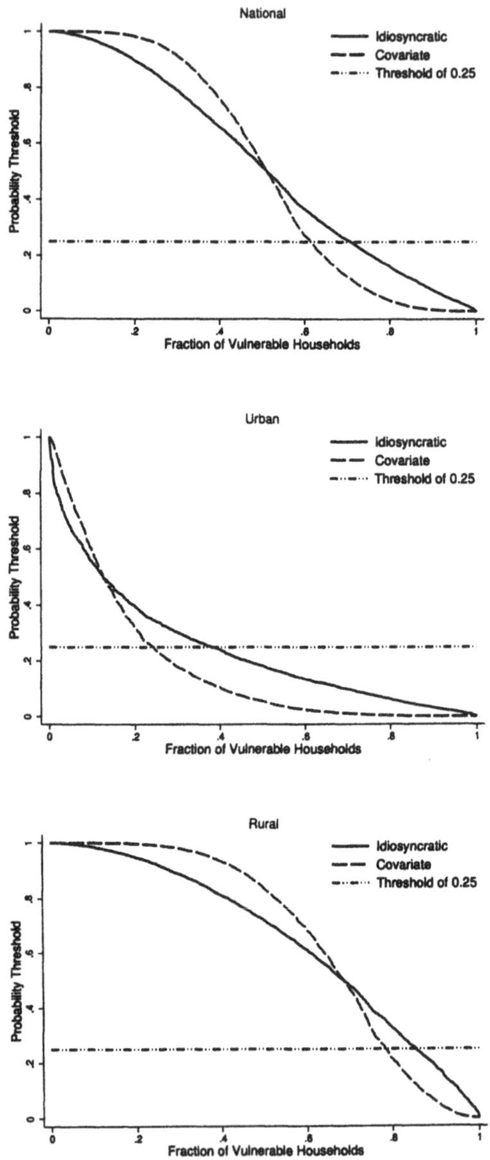


*Source:* ILO/Cornell Commune Level census 2001. *Enquete Auprès Des Menages*, 2001. Computations by the authors.

What is now interesting to see is that the relative importance of covariate and idiosyncratic shocks for rural and urban households' consumption depends on the vulnerability threshold chosen. The main reason for this result is that (i) vulnerability is an increasing (decreasing) function of consumption variance for a vulnerability threshold below (above) 0.50[25] and that (ii) for most households - irrespective of their mean consumption - idiosyncratic variance is higher than covariate variance in consumption.

## 3.5 Conclusion

We propose a simple method to analyze the level and sources of vulnerability using currently available standard cross-sectional or short panel household surveys without any explicit information on idiosyncratic and covariate shocks. Applying the concept of Chaudhuri (2002), defining vulnerability as the probability of a household to fall below the poverty line, we stated that both covariate and idiosyncratic shocks have a considerable impact on both urban and rural vulnerability. Furthermore, our results indicate that idiosyncratic shocks have an even higher impact on households' consumption volatility than covariate shocks and that idiosyncratic shocks seem to have a relatively higher impact on urban households' and covariate shocks a relatively higher impact on rural households' vulnerability.

It is difficult to assess whether a higher impact of certain types of shocks on rural or urban households' consumption is the result of a more severe impact of these shocks on households' income or the result of worse insurance mechanisms of households against these shocks. In other words, with the proposed method

[25]Note that with the assumption that consumption is log-normally distributed and with vulnerability defined as poverty risk, the estimated vulnerability of households with an expected mean consumption *above* the poverty line is an *increasing* function of consumption variance whereas the estimated vulnerability of households with an expected mean consumption *below* the poverty line is a *decreasing* function of consumption variance. In other words, households with a mean consumption above the poverty line and high variance in consumption face a high poverty-risk, whereas households with mean consumption below the poverty line and a high variance in consumption face a high probability escaping poverty, i.e. a 'lower' poverty risk. Hence, it might be useful to not only distinguish between 'structural' and 'risk induced'/'transitory' vulnerability but add a third category of the 'mobile poor', referring to poor households with a mean consumption below the poverty line but with high up-side potential. This is left for further research.

we can only assess the net (and not gross) impact of shocks on households' consumption. With these cautionary remarks in mind, we still provide some possible explanations for our results.

The suggested overall higher impact of idiosyncratic shocks on consumption volatility might first imply that insurance mechanisms within communities do not function any better than insurance mechanisms across communities. This would, however, be contradictory to micro-economic theory and some early empirical papers on consumption smoothing of idiosyncratic income fluctuations (e.g. Townsend, 1994, 1995). Or, and this fact has rarely been tested in the literature yet, idiosyncratic shocks might have a much higher impact on households' income than covariate shocks and even if mutual (but imperfect) insurance mechanisms are in place, still leading to higher consumption fluctuations than covariate shocks. Another alternative explanation could be that some covariate shocks are more anticipated than idiosyncratic shocks - because of a higher frequency and a higher correlation across years - so that *ex-ante* coping strategies take place. Both theories might be worthwhile to be tested empirically in further research.

The relatively higher impact of covariate shocks on rural households' consumption might be explained by the fact that there are certainly many more covariate shocks (such as climatic shocks) which have a higher impact on rural (agricultural) households than on urban (non-agricultural) households. It is further possible that urban households face higher information and enforcement limitations even within communities and that therefore informal insurance mechanisms against idiosyncratic shocks work better among rural than among urban households.

We also noted that the importance of consumption fluctuations (versus low mean consumption) seems to be even higher for urban households' welfare than for rural households' welfare. Hence, urban households should - if possible - be included into vulnerability studies, which have so far mostly focused on rural villages and households, ignoring the (increasing) urban population in developing countries.

We are aware of the fact that some rather stringent assumptions have to be made to estimate future variations in consumption based on data of only one single year. Therefore, the proposed approach should not be seen as an alternative to estimate vulnerability with lengthy panel data. However, we argue that as long as lengthy panel data with comprehensive information on idiosyncratic and covariate shocks is missing, the suggested approach can provide quite interesting insights into the relative impact of idiosyncratic and covariate shocks on households' vulnerability. Moreover, we recommend that any study which analyzes the influence of covariate shocks on households' consumption - no matter if cross-sectional or panel-data is used and independent of the extent of shock data available - should apply multilevel modeling as it appropriately takes into account the hierarchical structure of the data that is used for such analysis.

Last, it might be questioned whether estimated *ex-ante* poverty dynamics are *relevant* and *feasible* given the fact they have to be estimated with past data, which is often not even able to estimate *ex-post* poverty dynamics properly.[26] However, both from a policy and even more from a welfare perspective *future* poverty dynamics should have a higher relevance than *past* poverty dynamics. From a policy perspective, future poverty estimates are especially for targeting more important than past poverty estimates, as the households which are[27] or will be poor and not those which have been poor should be aided. From a welfare perspective, whereas both past as well as future poverty is important from a lifetime welfare perspective, future consumption prospects (or risks) might also have an impact on the *current* welfare of households which are risk-averse. How much weight future poverty dynamics should receive in present welfare estimates is open to discussion.

If we hence conclude that it is worthwhile to estimate *ex-ante* welfare dynamics, current living standard measurement surveys have to be improved to include (a better) time dimension, i.e. more precise data on past income, consumption, and asset fluctuations as well as on their causes and possibly also (subjective) information on welfare prospects.

[26]See also Essay 1.

[27]Poverty estimates are in general not available in the same year of the respective household survey, but because of data cleaning and processing in general with a one year delay.

# Essay 4

# A Competitive and Segmented Labor Market

*All models are wrong. Some of them are useful.*
G.E.P. Box, 1919-

**Abstract:** It has recently been argued that the informal sector in developing countries has a dual structure with part of the informal sector being competitive to the formal sector and part of the informal sector being the result of labor market segmentation. Although several authors have stressed this hypothesis of unobserved heterogeneity within the informal sector, this theory has so far not received satisfactory empirical treatment. In this paper, we formulate an econometric model which allows for a heterogenous informal sector with unobserved sector affiliation of individuals. Moreover, the model takes into account selection bias induced by the employment decision of individuals. Our empirical results for the urban labor market in Côte d'Ivoire show indeed the coexistence of competitive and segmented employment in the informal sector.

---

based on joint work with Andrey Launov.

# 4.1 Introduction

One often observed characteristic of urban labor markets in developing countries is the coexistence of a small formal sector with relatively high wages with a large informal sector with low and volatile earnings.[1] The role of the informal sector in the course of economic development was an extensively researched question in the 1970s (Fields, 1974; Hart, 1973; Livingstone, 1971; Mazumdar, 1976), when it became widely acknowledged that the informal sector was often the most important source of employment in developing countries, rather growing than shrinking as it would have been predicted by traditional dual economy theories (e.g. Lewis, 1954). Hence, in 1972 the International Labor Office (ILO) started to undertake studies especially focused on this sector of the labor market (ILO, 1972). Somewhat forgotten in the 1980s, at the end of the 1990s, with international development policy focusing on poverty reduction, the role of the informal sector, which is generally considered as the economy of the poor, reemerged on the policy and research agenda.

## 4.1.1 Theory of Informal Labor Markets

An important question both for the understanding of the informal sector as well as for policy recommendations is whether the observed differences in wages and working conditions in the formal and informal sector are the result of labor market segmentation or whether competitive labor market theories hold despite the observed differences in wages. A related question is whether individuals are poor because they are employed in the informal sector (segmented labor market), or whether they are employed in the informal sector because they are poor(ly endowed) with characteristics which generate high returns in the formal sector (competitive labor market).

Traditional dual labor market theories, which can be seen as a spin-off of dual economy theories (e.g. Lewis, 1954), assert that the informal sector is the disadvantaged sector into which workers enter to escape unemployment once they are rationed out of the formal sector where wages are set above market-clearing prices

[1] Besides low and volatile earnings, the informal sector can (among others) be characterized by small-scale enterprizes, labor-insensitivity, simple technology, ease of entry, family ownership and unregulated contracts and markets.

(Fields 1975; Harris and Todaro, 1970) for either institutional or efficiency-wage reasons (Stiglitz, 1976). Hence it is argued that workers in the informal sector, or the 'residual sector' of a segmented labor market, earn less than identical workers in the formal sector (see Figure 4.1). If no entry barriers existed, workers from the informal sector would enter the formal sector.

Figure 4.1: Segmented Labor Market

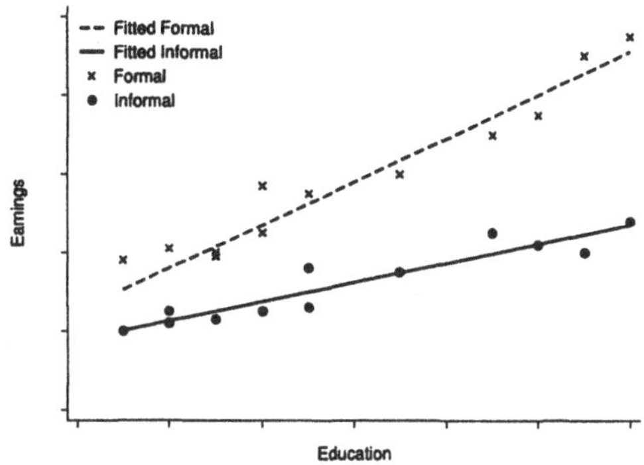


Figure 4.2: Competitive Labor Market

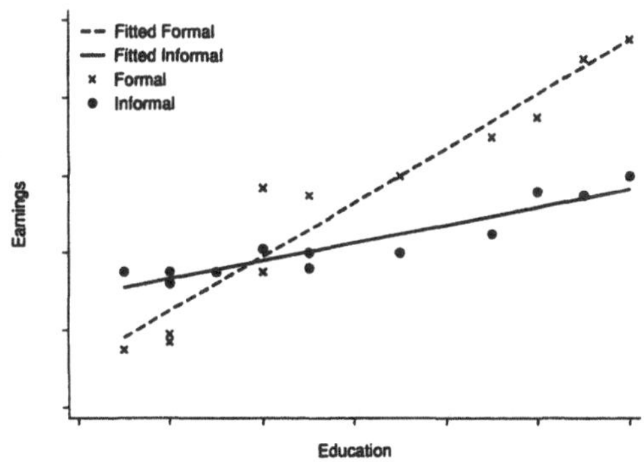


*Source:* Own Illustration.

While the sizable differences in earnings between the formal and informal sectors are uncontroversial, it has been claimed that the mere existence of lower wages and lower returns to education and experience in the informal sector does not yet imply market segmentation (see e.g. Dickens and Lang, 1985; Heckman and Hotz, 1986; Rosenzweig, 1988; Gindling, 1991; Maloney, 2004). More precisely, a labor market with two distinct wage equations does not constitute a segmented labor market as long as individuals are free to move between the two sectors .

An explanation for the existence of a formal and informal segment in the labor market would rather be that a large number of those working in the informal sector do so voluntarily, either because the informal sector has desirable non-wage features (Maloney, 2004) and individuals maximize their utility rather than their earnings, or because workers, given their characteristics, have a comparative advantage in the informal sector (e.g. Gindling, 1991) and would not do any better in the formal sector (see Figure 4.2).

Hence, two opposing theories exist. The segmentation hypothesis sees informal employment as a strategy of last resort to escape involuntary unemployment (Figure 4.1), whereas the comparative advantage hypothesis sees informal employment as a voluntary choice of workers based on income (or utility) maximization (Figure 4.2). This is nicely illustrated in Figures 4.1 and 4.2. In both figures average earnings as well as returns to education are lower in the informal than in the formal sector of the labor market. However, only in Figure 4.1 would all individuals (given their characteristics) earn more in the formal than in the informal sector, whereas this is not the case for Figure 4.2, where lower educated individuals earn more in the informal than in the formal sector. Hence, as long as we find the lower educated in the informal sector and the higher educated in the formal sector, earning differentials (as well as lower returns to education) do not constitute a segmented labor market but a competitive labor market, where individuals are found in the sector in which they have a comparative advantage.

Most recent theory on urban labor markets in developing countries has combined these polar views of competitive and segmented labor markets and emphasized a more complex structure of the informal sector, with an 'upper-tier' and 'lower-tier' or a 'voluntary entry' and 'involuntary entry' informal sector (Fields, 2005). The 'upper-tier' represents the competitive part into which individuals enter voluntarily because, given their specific characteristics, they expect to earn more than they would earn in the formal sector. The 'lower-tier', to the contrary, is the part that consists of individuals which were rationed out of the formal (and, possibly, 'upper-tier' informal) labor market.

### 4.1.2 Empirics of Informal Labor Markets

This latest theory is quite appealing as it could explain the inconclusive outcomes of several studies which have tried to test empirically whether formal-informal labor markets in developing countries are segmented or competitive. Among the most notable empirical contributions are Magnac (1990) and Gindling (1991). Magnac (1990) addresses the hypothesis of competitiveness in a framework of an extended Roy model whereas the paper of Gindling (1991) considers the same question in a framework of a generalized regression with sample selection introduced by Lee (1983). Both find weak evidence of a competitive rather than a segmented labor market structure.

In contrast, the latest hypothesis about competitive *and* segmented structure of the urban informal labor market has so far hardly received any empirical treatment. The difficulty of testing such a hypothesis is that the affiliation of any given individual to either part of the informal sector is unobservable, i.e. data on the causes of informal employment is in most cases missing. In addition, the selection bias that arises due to the non-random active population should be taken into account to get reliable estimates of expected earnings in both the formal sector as well as in any unobserved sector of the informal labor market (Heckman, 1979).

One of the very few empirical studies on a dual informal labor market has been undertaken by Cunningham and Maloney (2001), who represent the informal sector as a mixture of 'upper-tier' and 'lower-tier' enterprises. But as Cunningham and Maloney (2001) consider only informal entrepreneurs, an option of choosing formal sector employment does not even exist in their model. Moreover, unlike Magnac (1990) and Gindling (1991), Cunningham and Maloney (2001) do not consider selection bias induced by the employment decision of individuals. In this paper we hence suggest an econometric framework which is able to model the hypothesized heterogenous structure of the informal labor market as Cunningham and Maloney (2001) and at the same time considers sample selection bias as Magnac (1990) and Gindling (1991).

Following the argument of Fields (2005), we let the informal sector consist of a finite number of segments with unobservable sector affiliation of individuals and distinct earnings equations in each segment. Hence, the whole labor market is represented as a mixture model with both observable (for the formal sector) and unobservable (for the informal sector) membership. As the individual employment decision is influenced by the outside option of being non-employed, the earnings equations in each segment of the labor market should also depend on the labor market participation decision of individuals (Heckman, 1979). This leads to a finite mixture with sample selection, which allows us to estimate the distribution of individuals across different segments of the labor market as well as to estimate an unbiased earnings equation in each of them. Or in other words, we analyze whether the hypothesis of a dual informal sector can be supported by the data, and, if so, analyze the determinants of earnings in the two segments of the informal labor market.

Furthermore, we try to address the question if one part of the possibly detected heterogenous structure of the informal labor market is indeed the result of comparative advantage considerations whereas the other part is the result of entry barriers into the formal (and eventually also the competitive informal) labor market. Here we apply a quite simple and intuitive test. We assume that if individuals were earnings maximizers and could freely move between different parts of the labor market, the distribution of individuals across sectors induced by an earnings maximizing decision should be the same as the estimated distribution of individuals across sectors with the finite mixture model. Rejection of the equality of these two distributions implies the existence of entry barriers between different segments of the labor market, i.e. market segmentation.

The paper is structured as follows. Section 4.2 outlines the econometric model and constructs the test for market segmentation. Section 4.3 presents the data and the discussion of the empirical estimation results. Section 4.4 summarizes and concludes.

## 4.2 Econometric Model

We assume that the labor market consists of one formal and a finite number of unobservable informal sectors, with each sector having its own unique wage function. It is possible to empirically observe whether an individual does not participate in the labor market or belongs to the formal sector but impossible to observe affiliation to any of the latent segments of the informal sector. Workers are earnings maximizers and once they decide to become employed, knowledge of sector-specific wage functions allows them - given their characteristics - to form rational expectations about the wage they get in every sector. The labor market is competitive if there are no barriers to enter the sector which pays - conditional on workers' characteristics - the highest expected wage.

Below we develop an econometric model, which is a finite mixture with sample selection. Thus, we can test for unobserved informal sector heterogeneity as well as appropriately control for selection bias induced by the employment decision of individuals. Second, we formulate a test that allows to analyze whether informal employment is a result of market segmentation or comparative advantage considerations of individuals.

### 4.2.1 Specification

***Finite Mixture*** Assume that the labor market $Y$ consists of $J$ sectors $Y_j$ such that $Y = \bigcup_{j=1}^{J} Y_j$. Let earnings in each segment $Y_j$ be the outcome of a random variable with a probability distribution $F(y_j|\theta_j)$, where for all $j$, $F(y_j|\theta_j)$ are distinct and independent of each other. Next, assume that the affiliation of any individual earning $y_i$ to any segment $Y_j$ is unobservable. However, it is known that the probability of any individual earning $y_i$ to belong to $Y_j$ is given by $P(y \in Y_j) = \pi_j$. With these assumptions we can write the density of individual earnings $y_i$ as

$$f(y_i) = \sum_{j=1}^{J} f(y_i|\theta_j)\,\pi_j. \tag{4.1}$$

In other words, we suggest that the labor market consists of an arbitrary number of segments with a distinct earnings distribution in each of them and with unobserved sector affiliation of individual earnings. Our specification is hence a conventional mixture model. In this model the discrete mixing distribution $\{\pi_j\}_{j=1}^{J}$ is a parameter-free distribution of workers across all segments of the labor market. Each value $\pi_j$ can therefore be interpreted as the size of the $j$-th sector relative to the size of the whole market.

Next, assume that in any segment $Y_j$ of the labor market $Y$, the sector specific log-earnings are given by

$$\ln y_i = \mathbf{x}_i\beta_j + u_i, \quad u_i \sim N(0, \sigma_j^2 | y_i \in Y_j), \tag{4.2}$$

where $\mathbf{x}_i$ represents a set of personal characteristics. Using (4.1) and (4.2) it is easy to show that the expected log-earnings of any individual drawn from the whole population $Y$ are given by $E(\ln y_i) = \sum_{j=1}^{J} [\mathbf{x}_i\beta_j] \pi_j$. We can hence write down the earnings regression

$$\ln y_i = E(\ln y_i) + v_i, \quad y_i \in Y, \tag{4.3}$$

where the density of the error term $v_i$ is a mixture of standard normal densities

$$h(v_i) = \sum_{j=1}^{J} \frac{1}{\sigma_j} \varphi\left(\frac{\ln y_i - \mathbf{x}_i\beta_j}{\sigma_j}\right) \pi_j. \tag{4.4}$$

***Sample Selection*** One of the reasons why the regression in (4.3) might be misspecified is that earnings $y_i$ are only observed if an individual has decided to participate in the labor market. Being influenced by a subjective employment decision, the observed earnings sample may not necessarily be representative for the whole population (Heckman, 1979). This gives rise to sample selection bias.

If we assume that the employment decision of an individual depends on a set of personal characteristics $\mathbf{z}_i$, we can write down the following selection equation

$$y_{is} = \mathbf{z}_i\gamma + u_{is}, \quad u_{is} \sim N(0,1), \tag{4.5}$$

where $\mathbf{z}_i\gamma$ reflects the individual's decision to work. We can then state that wages $y_i$ in equation (4.2) are observed only if the realization of the selection variable $y_{is}$ is positive, i.e. whenever $u_{is} > -\mathbf{z}_i\gamma$.

Assuming that the errors of the $Y_j$-specific earnings equation (4.2) and the selection equation (4.5) follow a bivariate normal distribution with $Cov(u_i, u_{is}) = \rho_j\sigma_j$ we can represent the sample selection bias as an omitted variable in (4.3):

$$E(\ln y_i | y_{is} > 0) = E(\ln y_i) + \sum_{j=1}^{J} E(u_i | u_{is} > -\mathbf{z}_i\gamma; \mathbf{x}_i, \theta_j) \pi_j,$$

where $E(u_{ij} | u_{is} > -\mathbf{z}_i\gamma) \neq 0$ unless $\rho_j = 0$. Since $\sum_{j=1}^{J} E(u_i | u_{is} > -\mathbf{z}_i\gamma)$ is in general not equal to zero, the expected value of the error term $v_i$ in (4.3) will not be equal to zero. Thus the density of the error term in (4.4) will be misspecified. The selected-sample counterpart of the regression (4.3) is

$$\ln y_i = E(\ln y_i | y_{is} > 0) + v_i, \quad \{y_i \in Y : y_{is} > 0\} \tag{4.6}$$

and it can be shown that the density of the error term $v_i$ in (4.6) is a mixture density

$$\begin{aligned} h(v_i | y_{is} > 0) &= \sum_{j=1}^{J} h(u_i | \theta_j, y_{is} > 0)\, \pi_j \\ &= \sum_{j=1}^{J} \left[ \frac{\sigma_j^{-1}}{\Phi(\mathbf{z}_i \gamma)} \varphi \left( \frac{\ln y_i - \mathbf{x}_i \beta_j}{\sigma_j} \right) \Phi \left( \frac{\mathbf{z}_i \gamma + \rho_j \sigma_j^{-1} [\ln y_i - \mathbf{x}_i \beta_j]}{\left(1 - \rho_j^2\right)^{1/2}} \right) \right] \pi_j, \end{aligned} \tag{4.7}$$

where $\varphi$ and $\Phi$ are the standard normal density and distribution functions.[2] The above mixture model is a generalization of Heckman regression with sample selection that allows for $J$ different conditional distributions of the dependent variable instead of only one.

The model in (4.7) is only identifiable, i.e. it rules out the existence of two distinct mixtures that have the same probability law for the observed dependent variable $Y_i$, if $\rho_j = \rho \forall j = 1, ..., J$.

**Proposition 1** *For any given selection rule $\{\mathbf{Z}, \gamma\}$, the finite mixture (4.7) is identifiable if $\rho_j = \rho$, $\forall j = 1, ..., J$.*

**Proof.** *We verify the Teicher (1963) sufficient condition for identifiability of finite mixtures (see Appendix B).* ■

Thus, the general class of finite mixtures with sample selection is not identifiable. So we should focus on a sub-class where the correlation between the errors of the selection and earnings equations is the same for every segment of the labor market, i.e. $\rho_j = \rho$, $\forall j = 1, ..., J$. This result is however rather of a statistical nature, as setting $\rho_j = \rho$ implies no artificial economic restrictions to the model.[3]

[2] Derivation of the component density of this mixture is presented in Appendix B.

[3] The main interpretation of $\rho_j$ is a statistical one of $\rho_j$ indicating the importance of model selection for analyzing earnings equations, i.e. mapping the correlation between the selection and the earnings equation. In Appendix B, Remark 1, it is furthermore shown that the proof of Proposition 1 also implies the assumption of a common selection rule $\gamma_j = \gamma$, $\forall j = 1, ...J$. This means that individuals with the same characteristics have the same probability to participate in the labor market - independent of the segment they will later be found in if employed.

The specification of the error distribution in the regression on a selected sample of earnings (4.6) therefore becomes

$$h(v_i|\theta,\rho) = \sum_{j=1}^{J}\left[\frac{\sigma_j^{-1}}{\Phi(\mathbf{z}_i\gamma)}\varphi\left(\frac{\ln y_i - \mathbf{x}_i\beta_j}{\sigma_j}\right)\Phi\left(\frac{\mathbf{z}_i\gamma+\rho\sigma_j^{-1}\left[\ln y_i - \mathbf{x}_i\beta_j\right]}{(1-\rho^2)^{1/2}}\right)\right]\pi_j, \tag{4.8}$$

where $\theta = \left\{\beta_j,\sigma_j\right\}_{j=1}^{J}$. This model allows for a labor market with multiple segments where individuals' sector affiliation is unobserved. Moreover the model accounts for the subjective employment decision of individuals. Thus we can analyze whether a model with a latent heterogenous structure of the informal labor market, as suggested by Fields (2005), can better explain observed earnings in the labor market than traditional models with a homogenous informal sector.

### 4.2.2 Test for Segmentation or Competitiveness

The above formulated model also suggests a simple test to analyze whether the 'revealed' distribution of individuals across the sectors of the labor market is a result of market segmentation or a result of comparative advantage considerations.

Assume that workers are earnings maximizers and every worker knows the wage function in each sector, and hence - given his own characteristics - his expected wage in each sector. Let $y_i^j$ denote the earnings of individual $i$ in sector $j$. Given the above assumptions, competitive theory would imply that an individual - knowing the wage function in each sector - would be found in the sector where his expected earnings - given his personal characteristics - are maximized. The probability distribution of individuals across sectors would then become

$$P(y \in Y_j) = P\left(E\left[\ln y^j | y_s > 0; \mathbf{x}\right] = \max_{l,l\neq j}\left\{E\left[\ln y^l | y_s > 0; \mathbf{x}\right]\right\}\right). \tag{4.9}$$

Equation (4.9) provides us with a 'hypothetical' distribution of individuals across sectors.[4] This distribution is conditional on individual characteristics and rests on the assumption that there are no barriers to enter the sector that pays the highest expected wage. Hence Equation (4.9) provides us with the distribution of individuals across sectors if the market were competitive. On the other hand, the

[4]Details on the computation of Equation (4.9) are presented in Appendix B.

'actual' distribution of individuals across sectors is given by the mixing distribution $\{\pi_j\}_{j=1}^J$ in equation (4.8). This distribution is independent of wage functions in any sector and relies on no assumptions regarding entry barriers.

An equal distribution of individuals across sectors induced by the mixing probabilities $\{\pi_j\}_{j=1}^J$ in (4.8) and induced by individuals' optimal sector choice as described in (4.9) indicates perfect mobility between the various sectors of the labor market, i.e. a competitive market. In contrast, if the 'actual' mixing distribution in (4.8) and the 'hypothetical' distribution in (4.9) differ significantly from each other, entry-barriers between the sectors seem to prevent some individuals entering the sector that pays them the highest expected wage. Hence we would face a segmented labor market.

### 4.2.3 Implementation

To estimate the above described model we suggest the following two-step procedure:

Step 1: Estimate $\gamma$ in the selection equation (4.5) by running a Probit.

Step 2: Use $\mathbf{z}_i\hat{\gamma}$ as consistent estimates of $\mathbf{z}_i\gamma$ to estimate the model in (4.8).

Typically we can observe from the data whether an individual belongs to the formal sector. So, only the affiliation to the latent segments of the informal sector remains unobservable. Denote the set of earnings outcomes in the formal sector by $Y_F$ and the number of observations in the formal sector by $N_F$. Using (4.8), the log-likelihood is

$$\ln \mathscr{L}_L = \sum_{i \in Y_F} \ln h_i\left(\theta_F, \rho | y_i, \mathbf{x}_i, \mathbf{z}_i\hat{\gamma}\right) - N_F \ln \pi_F + \sum_{i \notin Y_F} \left[ \ln \left( \sum_{j=1}^{J-1} h_i\left(\theta_{I.j}, \rho | y_i, \mathbf{x}_i, \mathbf{z}_i\hat{\gamma}\right) \pi_{I.j} \right) \right], \tag{4.10}$$

where $\pi_F$ is the probability of belonging to the formal sector, $\pi_{I.j}$ is a probability of belonging to the $j$-th segment of the informal sector and $h_i\left(\theta_j, \rho\right)$ is a component density from (4.8). It is also straightforward to show that a maximum likelihood (ML) estimate of $\pi_F$ is equal to the share of formal workers in the whole sample.

The asymptotic covariance matrix of the estimates of the second step vector of the parameters $\xi = \left\{ \{\theta_j\}_{j=1}^{J}, \rho, \{\pi_{I,j}\}_{j=1}^{J-1} \right\}$ is given by

$$V(\xi) = D^{-1}(\xi) + D^{-1}(\xi) M(\xi,\gamma) D^{-1}(\xi), \tag{4.11}$$

where $D(\xi)$ is the expected negative Hessian and $M(\xi,\gamma)$ is the matrix constructed using the scores from the first and second steps (for the exact form of $M(\xi,\gamma)$, see Murphy and Topel, 1985).

Note that a full information maximum likelihood estimation is also possible. In this case the log-likelihood function becomes

$$\ln \mathscr{L}_F = \ln \mathscr{L}_L(\xi,\gamma) + \sum_{i \in Y^c} \ln(1 - \Phi(\mathbf{z}_i\gamma)), \tag{4.12}$$

where $\ln \mathscr{L}_L$ is the log-likelihood function in (4.10) with $\gamma$ as an unknown parameter vector and $Y^c$ denotes the complementary set of non-employed individuals.

## 4.3 Empirical Application

### 4.3.1 Data Description

The data we use is drawn from the 1998[5] Ivorian household survey, the *Enquête de Niveau de Vie*, which was undertaken by the *Institut National de la Statistique de la Côte d'Ivoire* and the World Bank. We focus our analysis on the urban population and limit our sample to individuals between the age of 15 and 65 years. This leaves us with a sample of 5592 observations. Among these, we consider those individuals as inactive who voluntarily stay out of the labor market as well as those who are involuntarily unemployed, as this is only a very small share of the inactive population.[6]

The active population is classified into the informal and formal sector according to reported primary employment.[7] The formal sector includes individuals

[5] We used a rather dated survey of Côte d'Ivoire to exclude the adverse effects of the Ivorian crisis since 2001.

[6] Only 11.3 percent of the inactive population are looking for employment.

[7] Consideration of secondary informal employment of employees in the formal sector, which is an often observed characteristic of urban labor markets in developing countries, would imply that the earnings distributions in $Y_F$ and $Y_I$ are no longer independent. An extension of the model that incorporates this fact is left for future research.

working in the public sector as well as wage workers and self-employed in the formal private sector. As formal private we consider being employed in an enterprise which either pursues formal bookkeeping and/or offers written contracts and/or pay slips. The informal sector comprises the active population which is neither employed in the public nor in the private formal sector.

Figure 4.3: Densities of Monthly Earnings

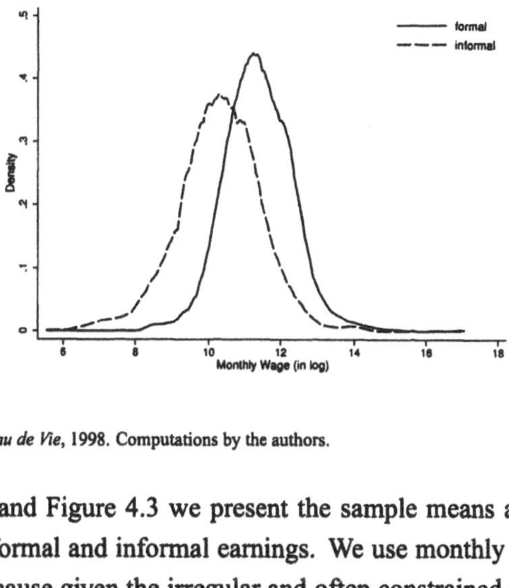


*Source: Enquête de Niveau de Vie*, 1998. Computations by the authors.

In Table 4.1 and Figure 4.3 we present the sample means and kernel densities of monthly formal and informal earnings. We use monthly wages instead of hourly wages because given the irregular and often constrained working hours in the informal sector we think that monthly wages reflect earning opportunities in the informal sector better than hourly wages. As expected, there is a large earnings differential between informal (64,837 CFA per month) and formal (164,995 CFA per month) workers. However, Figure 4.3 also demonstrates that despite the considerable difference in mean earnings, the densities of informal and formal earnings overlap to a large extent, already indicating that not all informal employment is inferior to all formal employment.

Table 4.1 also displays summary statistics of the variables used in the earnings equations. The information is provided for the population as a whole as well as separately for inactive workers and workers in the informal and formal sectors respectively. The educational level is the highest in the formal sector (8.1 years),

Table 4.1: Summary Statistics of the Urban Labor Market

| | Total* | Inactive | Active | |
|---|---|---|---|---|
| | | | Informal | Formal |
| Sample | 100% | 52.6% | 31.3% | 16.1% |
| Monthly earnings | 98,815 | – | 64,837 | 164,995 |
| Male | 49.7% | 40.6% | 49.0% | 80.6% |
| Age (in years) | 30.0 | 25.2 | 34.7 | 36.6 |
| Education (in years) | 5.3 | 5.8 | 2.9 | 8.1 |
| Literacy rate | 64.1% | 69.8% | 44.4% | 84.0% |
| Training after school (yes=1) | 17.6% | 11.1% | 14.7% | 44.3% |
| Religion | | | | |
| Muslim | 43.4% | 38.3% | 56.8% | 33.8% |
| Christian | 42.2% | 46.2% | 30.6% | 52.2% |
| Indigenous | 14.4% | 15.5% | 12.6% | 14.0% |
| Living in Abidjan | 49.6% | 50.4% | 42.2% | 61.7% |

*Source: Enquête de Niveau de Vie*, 1998. Computations by the authors.
*Notes:* Monthly earnings in CFA Francs. *) 'Total' refers to individuals between 15 and 65 years of age.

with somewhat lower and much lower educational attainment among inactive (5.8 years) and informal (2.9 years) workers. With regard to age, we find the youngest individuals among the inactive (mean age of 25.2 years) followed by informal (34.7 years) and formal (36.6 years) employees. In addition, membership in the formal sector is a privilege of males, who constitute 80.6 percent of formal employees. In contrast, only 49.0 percent of informal workers and 40.6 percent of inactive individuals are males.

Finally, an interesting observation can be made about the distribution of religious groups in the active population: despite the same fraction of Muslims and Christians in the entire sample, the formal sector is dominated by Christians whereas the informal sector is dominated by Muslims. This can first be caused by the specific composition of the government, i.e. the public sector, which constitutes a large part of the formal sector and which is dominated by Christians. An alternative 'geographic' explanation might be that formal employment is predominantly concentrated in the Southern cities - especially in Abidjan - where most

Christians live, whereas Muslims are rather living in the Northern part of Côte d'Ivoire.

Hence, there are considerable differences in characteristics between both the inactive and active population as well as between workers employed in the informal and formal sectors. Systematic differences between active and inactive individuals highlights the possible sample selection bias, that may arise if we ignore the employment decision of individuals in our model. The nature of systematic differences in characteristics of formal and informal workers is a bit less clear. It might be the result of self-selection of employees into the sectors where they maximize their earnings as well as the result of employers' discrimination based on workers' characteristics.

To specify the selection equation we use other variables such as the number of infants in the household, the number of children under 14 in the household, the number of old household members, household size and the number of active members in the household. The reason for this choice is twofold. First, the above listed variables filter out non-individual reasons for making job decision, such as family and environment matters, so that the magnitude of the earnings could be later explained by only individual qualities. Second, these variables provide sufficient exclusion restrictions advocated by Olsen (1980) and Little (1985) for Heckman regressions.

### 4.3.2 Heterogenous Informal Labor Markets

We start with an analysis of the sector composition of the labor market. The econometric model described in Section 4.2 allows for an arbitrary number of (finite) labor market segments where individual affiliation to any of them is not necessarily observable.[8] Initially we estimate two specifications: a model with a homogeneous informal sector and a model with an informal sector that consists of two segments (see Table 4.4). To decide on the number of segments in the

[8]Moreover, the model takes into account selectivity induced by individuals' employment decision, which ensures consistent estimation of marginal returns to individual characteristics in each sector of the labor market.

labor market we use information criteria:[9] Akaike, Schwarz, consistent Akaike and Hannan-Quinn. The results on model selection are presented in Table 4.2. All information criteria uniformly show that the specification with a dual informal sector is superior to the model with a homogeneous informal sector. Thus the labor market under study consists of at least three distinct parts: the formal sector and two latent segments of the informal sector.

Table 4.2: Model Selection - Total Urban Labor Market

| | Homogeneous Informal Sector | Two-Segment Informal Sector | Three-Segment Informal Sector |
|---|---|---|---|
| Akaike | 13708.12 | ***13610.56*** | 13610.73 |
| Schwarz | 13835.38 | ***13808.40*** | 13879.27 |
| Consistent Akaike | 13921.59 | ***13906.60*** | 13989.47 |
| Hannan-Quinn | 13774.16 | ***13702.09*** | 13727.90 |
| $\ln \mathscr{L}_L$ | -5332.92 | -5272.11 | -5260.23 |
| $\ln \mathscr{L}_F$ | -6823.06 | -6762.25 | -6750.37 |

*Source: Enquête de Niveau de Vie*, 1998. Computations by the authors.
*Notes:* $\ln \mathscr{L}_L$ is the log-likelihood from the second step and $\ln \mathscr{L}_F$ is the log-likelihood from the full model. All information criteria are based on $\ln \mathscr{L}_F$. However, our conclusions would not change if we based the information criteria on $\ln \mathscr{L}_L$.

Extending the model to a three-segment informal sector does not lead to an improvement in terms of information criteria. From the last column of Table 4.2 we see that all information criteria show that such a specification would overparameterize the model. In addition, the extended three-segment model would place a very low probability (i.e. size) on the third segment of the informal market. The estimated size of this additional segment would only be 4.1 percent of the informal sector and 2.7 percent of the whole labor market respectively. We hence conclude that the specification with a two-segment informal labor market is the best fitting and simultaneously most parsimonious model.

[9]Using information criteria is the only feasible way to decide on the appropriate specification. Since the component densities in (4.8) do not belong to the exponential family, the residual-based methods for selecting the optimal mixture (see Lindsay and Roeder, 1992) cannot be applied here.

We also estimate the model with a homogenous and a heterogenous informal sector separately for the 'male' and 'female' urban labor market,[10] as it is often argued that there is a gender-specific division of the labor market in developing countries and especially in sub-Saharan Africa (see e.g. Klasen, 2006 for an overview). Hence, we test if the result of a two-segment informal labor market is dependent on whether we estimate the model for the total urban population or for males and females separately.

Table 4.3 demonstrates, that only two out of four information criteria indicate that the male informal labor market has a heterogenous structure and two information criteria would suggest that the specification with a homogeneous informal sector is best. For the female labor market the model with a heterogenous informal labor market is supported by three out of four information criteria whereas Consistent Akaike is inconclusive (Table 4.3). Hence, the informal labor market of males might - in contrast to the informal labor market of females - be homogenous. Moreover, the results indicate that part of the strong heterogenous structure of the overall informal labor market (Table 4.2) might be caused by a gender-specific division.

Table 4.3: Model Selection - Male and Female Urban Labor Market

| | Males | | Females | |
|---|---|---|---|---|
| | Homogeneous Informal Sector | Two-Segment Informal Sector | Homogenous Informal Sector | Two-Segment Informal Sector |
| Akaike | 6243.16 | ***6202.06*** | 4107.97 | ***4053.74*** |
| Schwarz | ***6383.26*** | 6412.22 | 4250.86 | ***4239.39*** |
| Consistent Akaike | ***6361.26*** | 6379.22 | 4217.39 | 4217.86 |
| Hannan-Quinn | 6287.03 | ***6267.88*** | 4149.42 | ***4115.92*** |

*Source: Enquête de Niveau de Vie*, 1998. Computations by the authors.

Estimation results for the total urban labor market and for the model with a two-segment informal labor market are presented in Table 4.4. Considering the

[10] The respective earnings regressions of Table 4.4 for male and female workers separately are not shown as they do not provide any additional insights above the results stated in Table 4.4.

estimation results, our first important finding is that the correlation coefficient between the selection equation and the earnings equations is significant, which underlines the necessity of accounting for sample selection bias when estimating coefficients in segment-specific earnings equations.[11]

With regard to the characteristics of each segment of the labor market, Table 4.4 suggests that expected wages in both informal segments are clearly below the expected wage in the formal sector. However, there is an additional significant differential between expected earnings in the higher-paid (Informal-1) and lower-paid (Informal-2) informal sectors.[12] Moreover, the two unobserved informal segments make up 37.7 percent (Informal-1) and 28.4 percent (Informal-2) of the labor market, or 57.6 percent and 42.4 percent of the informal labor market respectively, which shows that each of them constitutes a significant part of the informal sector (Table 4.4).[13]

Last, notice that wage equations across the three segments are quite diverse. As expected, returns to education and experience (measured in years of age) are high in the formal sector. Also, in the higher-paid segment of the informal sector (Informal-1) education and experience have a high and significant impact on earnings. But, whereas returns to experience in this segment are the same as in the formal sector, returns to education are only half as high. In the lower-paid part of the informal sector (Informal-2) returns to experience are only two thirds of the returns to experience in the formal and higher-paid informal sectors, and education appears to have no returns at all. Hence, workers in the lower-paid informal sector are stuck with very low wages almost independent of their abilities

[11] The correlation coefficient $\rho$ is also significant whether we estimate the model separately for males or females (not shown).

[12] As indicated by the coefficient on the impact of gender on earnings, if we estimate the model only for female employees the wage differential between the formal and higher-paid informal sector is higher whereas it is lower between the higher-paid and lower-paid informal sector.

[13] If we estimate the model for males only the respective shares are 32.7 (Informal-1) and 21.0 (Informal-2) percent of the labor market whereas for the female labor market the shares amount up to 44.7 (Informal-1) and 39.0 (Informal-2) percent, respectively. Hence, not only is the share of women working in the informal sector much higher, but especially the share of women working in the lower-paid informal sector is much higher than the share of males working in this - with regard to expected earnings - most-disadvantaged sector.

Table 4.4: Regression Results for log Earnings

| **Formal** | Coeff. | (Std.Error) | **Informal 1** | Coeff. | (Std.Error) | **Informal 2** | Coeff. | (Std.Error) |
|---|---|---|---|---|---|---|---|---|
| Intercept* | 7.0516 | 0.3799 | Intercept* | 7.5818 | 0.3225 | Intercept* | 7.4643 | 0.5803 |
| Male* | 0.3476 | 0.0734 | Male* | 0.6659 | 0.0700 | Male* | 0.4417 | 0.1257 |
| Age* | 0.1301 | 0.0196 | Age* | 0.1199 | 0.0169 | Age* | 0.0816 | 0.0307 |
| $Age^2$/100* | −0.1187 | 0.0258 | $Age^2$/100* | −0.1285 | 0.0221 | $Age^2$/100* | −0.1012 | 0.0397 |
| Education* | 0.1058 | 0.0091 | Education* | 0.0577 | 0.0160 | Education | 0.0210 | 0.0261 |
| Literacy | −0.1420 | 0.1140 | Literacy | −0.1405 | 0.1103 | Literacy | 0.0706 | 0.1958 |
| Training* | 0.1600 | 0.0626 | Training | −0.1190 | 0.1063 | Training* | 0.6664 | 0.2031 |
| Muslim | 0.1550 | 0.0896 | Muslim | −0.0923 | 0.0979 | Muslim* | 0.7532 | 0.2103 |
| Christian | −0.0185 | 0.0850 | Christian | −0.0505 | 0.1025 | Christian | 0.4026 | 0.2150 |
| Abidjan | 0.0807 | 0.0576 | Abidjan* | 0.1871 | 0.0683 | Abidjan* | 0.2530 | 0.1225 |
| $\pi_F^*$ : | 0.3392 | 0.0092 | $\pi_{I.1}^*$ : | 0.3767 | 0.0403 | $\pi_{I.2}^*$ : | 0.2840 | 0.0401 |
| Exp. log-Wage: | 11.3524 | | Exp. log-Wage: | 10.4956 | | Exp. log-Wage: | 10.0964 | |
| Exp. Wage: | 105095.04 | | Exp. Wage: | 40992.12 | | Exp. Wage: | 28054.92 | |
| **Selection Equation** | | | | | | | | |
| Intercept | −0.0422 | 0.0400 | Number of Obs. (cens): | 2939 | | | | |
| Male* | 0.5682 | 0.0374 | Number of Obs. (mix): | 2653 | | | | |
| Infants* | 0.2705 | 0.0196 | | | | | | |
| Children* | 0.2677 | 0.0162 | Log-Likelihood: | −5272.11 | | | | |
| Olds | −0.0518 | 0.0439 | $\rho$ * | 0.1058 | | | | |
| HH Size* | −0.2693 | 0.0092 | | | | | | |
| Active Members* | 0.4709 | 0.0157 | | | | | | |

*Source:* *Enquête de Niveau de Vie*, 1998. Computations by the authors.

*Notes:* * denotes significance at 5% level.

Furthermore, whereas gender has a considerable impact on earnings in all segments of the labor market, the male-female wage gap in the two informal segments is much higher than in the formal sector. An explanation could be, that positions in the formal sector are much more specified, preventing high gender-specific wage discrimination. Alternatively, it is also possible that only the most (unobserved) able females enter the formal labor market, leading to a lower difference in earnings in the formal sector. Last, both location and religion does not have an impact on earnings in the formal sector but does have a significant impact on earnings in the better- and lower-paid informal sector.

Thus we do not only find that the urban labor market in Côte d'Ivoire consists of one formal and two latent informal segments. Also, each of these segments shows a quite distinct pattern of returns to individual characteristics. On a first glance, among the different labor market theories (as described in the introduction), the proposed labor market structure of Fields (2005) seems to be supported most by our empirical results.

However, even a significant diversity in the characteristics of the different labor market segments does not necessarily mean that the labor market does not fit into either the segmented or the competitive labor market model. Following Basu (1997), it is beyond doubts that the labor market may be split into several segments. But as long as these segments possess the properties attributable to a competitive market, the whole labor market can still be treated as competitive. Alternatively, if entry barriers between some detected fragments could be found, the market would be segmented. Thus, to learn about the nature of segmentation and/or competition in the labor market, it has to be analyzed whether the observed distribution of individuals across segments is the result of sector choice (competitive market) or entry-barriers into sectors (segmented market).

### 4.3.3 Competitive or Segmented Labor Markets?

In this section we analyze whether employment in the two informal segments is the result of own comparative advantage considerations or a result of entry-barriers into the formal market, i.e. market segmentation. If no entry-barriers between sectors exist the 'earnings-maximizing' individual enters the sector where, given his characteristics, his expected earnings are the highest. This induces the distribution of individuals across sectors formulated in Equation (4.9), which we could call the 'earnings-maximizing' distribution across sectors $\{\tilde{\pi}_j\}_{j=1}^J$. Without entry-barriers the earnings-maximizing distribution should be the same as the actual distribution of individuals across sectors, i.e. the mixing distribution $\{\hat{\pi}_j\}_{j=1}^J$ in Equation (4.8).[14]

If, however, certain entry-barriers are in place, individuals should be underrepresented in the sectors where they would have the highest expected earnings (given their specific characteristics). Or in other words, if entry-barriers existed, there should be a statistically significant difference between the estimated actual mixing distribution and the distribution induced by the earnings-maximizing sector choice of individuals.

Figure 4.4: Distribution of Individuals across Sectors

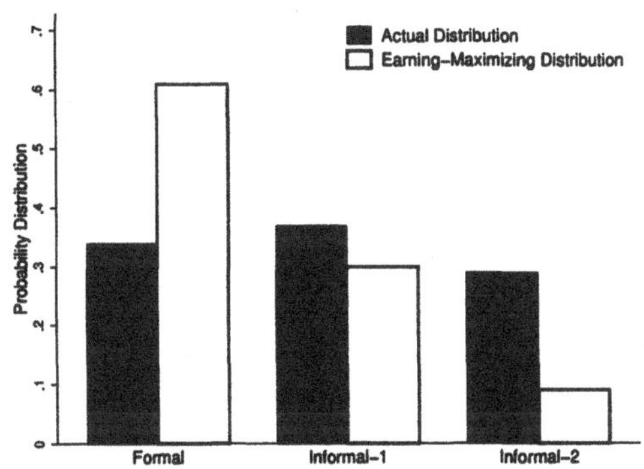


*Source: Enquête de Niveau de Vie*, 1998. Computations by the authors.

Figure 4.4 plots the detected market segments from the mixture model $\{\hat{\pi}_j\}_{j=1}^J$ against the earnings-maximizing distribution $\{\tilde{\pi}_j\}_{j=1}^J$. We see that the fraction of those who, conditional on their personal characteristics, would be better off in the formal sector is almost double the actual share of formal sector employees. The contrary can be observed in the lower-paid informal segment, where the actual

[14]See also Section 4.2.2. Note that the term 'actual' here refers to 'estimated' and may not be confused with the term 'perfectly observable', because we are in the mixture setting and the affiliation of an informal worker to any part of the informal sector is unobservable.

number of workers is almost three times as high as the number of workers that would choose to be employed in this segment for comparative advantage considerations.

Table 4.5: Distribution of Individuals across Sectors

| | | Formal | | Informal-1 | | Informal-2 | |
|---|---|---|---|---|---|---|---|
| | | Value | [95% Conf.Int.] | Value | [95% Conf.Int.] | Value | [95% Conf.Int.] |
| Actual | $\hat{\pi}_j$ | 0.33 | [0.32, 0.35] | 0.37 | [0.23, 0.48] | 0.28 | [0.17, 0.42] |
| Maximizing | $\tilde{\pi}_j$ | 0.61 | [0.37, 0.77] | 0.29 | [0.14, 0.52] | 0.09 | [0.03, 0.18] |
| Actual/Maximizing | $\hat{\pi}_j/\tilde{\pi}_j$ | 0.55 | [0.43, 0.92] | 1.28 | [0.52, 3.14] | 3.03 | [1.20, 8.59] |

*Source: Enquête de Niveau de Vie*, 1998. Computations by the authors.
*Notes:* 'Actual' denotes the actual mixing distribution, whereas 'Maximizing' denotes the estimated earnings-maximizing distribution. [95% Conf.Int.] denotes a 95% Confidence Interval.

Table 4.5 presents the corresponding estimated values of the actual mixing, $\{\hat{\pi}_j\}_{j=1}^{J}$, and earnings-maximizing, $\{\tilde{\pi}_j\}_{j=1}^{J}$, sector affiliation probabilities as well as the ratios of these values for each segment $j$. In addition, we report the bootstrap confidence intervals for the estimated probabilities and for their ratios. The hypothesis of equality of the two distributions is rejected when the $\hat{\pi}_j/\tilde{\pi}_j$ ratios significantly diverge from unity.

The results in Table 4.5 indicate that the actual sector affiliation probability is significantly different from the earnings-maximizing affiliation probability both for the formal sector and the lower-paid informal sector (Informal-2) and only equal for the higher-paid informal sector (Informal-1). More precisely, at a 5% significance level we find that $\hat{\pi}_j/\tilde{\pi}_j = 1$ for the higher-paid informal sector, $\hat{\pi}_j/\tilde{\pi}_j < 1$ for the formal sector and $\hat{\pi}_j/\tilde{\pi}_j > 1$ for the lower-paid informal sector. These findings imply:

(i) the share of workers who would choose to enter the formal sector is significantly higher than the share of workers indeed employed in the formal sector,

(ii) the actual share of individuals affiliated to the Informal-1 sector is equal to the share of those who would optimally choose working in this sector,

(iii) the actual share of workers in the Informal-2 sector is significantly higher than the share of workers that would voluntarily stay in this sector.

The three statements above clearly imply the rejection of the hypothesis of unlimited inter-sectoral mobility with no entry-barriers between any sectors. Thus, the labor market under study is segmented and features involuntary employment, mainly in its lower-paid informal segment, where a significant fraction of workers would do better in another sector (Table 4.5). This means that competitive theories do not apply. Moreover, our results do neither support full labor market segmentation, that considers all informal employment as a strategy of last resort to escape involuntary unemployment. Figure 4.4 and Table 4.5 show that both informal segments, mainly Informal-1 but also Informal-2, also contain individuals who will not be better off in any other sector. Thus the informal market seems to consist of both workers who are employed there voluntary - the upper-tier - and involuntary - the lower-tier. Hence, we conclude that the hypothesis of Fields (2005) can largely be supported.

More precisely, the earnings-maximizing distribution $\{\tilde{\pi}_j\}_{j=1}^{J}$ of Informal-1 and Informal-2 constitutes the upper-tier, i.e. individuals who voluntary work in the informal sector and would not be better off in any other sector. The difference between these earnings-maximizing individuals in the informal sector and the actual size of the informal sector indicates the lower-tier informal sector, i.e. individuals who involuntary work in the informal sector and would do better in the formal sector. Table 4.5 shows that the relative size of the lower-tier informal sector is about 27% of the entire labor market[15] or about 40% of the informal sector and that those individuals are mainly found in the lower-paid informal sector (Informal-2). The higher-tier informal segment makes up 60 % of the informal labor market and is mainly found in the upper-paid informal segment (Informal-1).

Table 4.6 shows the actual mixing $\hat{\pi}_j$ and the predicted earnings-maximizing probabilities $\tilde{\pi}_j$ separately for males and females. With regard to the labor market of males, only 14% of males are not found in the sector where they would maximize their earnings, or in other words the size of the lower-tier informal sector is about 25% of the 'male' informal labor market. For females, 17% (20%) of the 'female' total (informal) labor market are found in the lower-tier informal sector.

[15]This is equal to the difference between the actual and earnings-maximizing fractions of workers employed in the formal sector.

These in the lower-tier involuntary trapped women and men are almost exclusively found in the lower-paid informal sector, Informal-2 (see column 2 and 3 of Table 4.6).[16] Thus, if we analyze the female and male labor market separately most individuals seem to be in the sector where they maximize their earnings, which indicates 'gender-specific' competitive labor markets; and hence, in combination with the results of the total labor market (Table 4.5), a partly 'gender-driven' labor market segmentation.

Table 4.6: Distribution of Individuals across Sectors - Males and Females

| | | Males | | | | | |
|---|---|---|---|---|---|---|---|
| | | Formal | | Informal-1 | | Informal-2 | |
| | | Value | [95% Conf.Int.] | Value | [95% Conf.Int.] | Value | [95% Conf.Int.] |
| Actual | $\hat{\pi}_j$ | 0.45 | [0.43, 0.48] | 0.32 | [0.12, 0.50] | 0.21 | [0.03, 0.40] |
| Maximizing | $\tilde{\pi}_j$ | 0.60 | [0.12, 0.71] | 0.32 | [0.12, 0.83] | 0.06 | [0.01, 0.27] |
| Actual/Maximizing | $\hat{\pi}_j/\tilde{\pi}_j$ | 0.75 | [0.63, 3.78] | 0.99 | [0.22, 3.98] | 3.31 | [0.36, 6.81] |
| | | Females | | | | | |
| | | Formal | | Informal-1 | | Informal-2 | |
| | | Value | [95% Conf.Int.] | Value | [95% Conf.Int.] | Value | [95% Conf.Int.] |
| Actual | $\hat{\pi}_j$ | 0.16 | [0.14, 0.18] | 0.44 | [0.23, 0.75] | 0.39 | [0.07, 0.61] |
| Maximizing | $\tilde{\pi}_j$ | 0.32 | [0.22, 0.81] | 0.45 | [0.07, 0.65] | 0.21 | [0.06, 0.38] |
| Actual/Maximizing | $\hat{\pi}_j/\tilde{\pi}_j$ | 0.49 | [0.19, 0.74] | 0.98 | [0.37, 4.86] | 1.80 | [0.30, 7.37] |

*Source: Enquête de Niveau de Vie*, 1998. Computations by the authors.
*Notes:* 'Actual' denotes the actual mixing distribution, whereas 'Maximizing' denotes the estimated earnings-maximizing distribution. [95% Conf.Int.] denotes a 95% Confidence Interval.

One might argue, that in reality individuals are utility- rather than earnings-maximizers. Thus, it is possible to argue that our empirical results are a consequence of non-wage preferences for the lower-paid informal sector and not an

[16] The actual size of the higher-paid informal sector, Informal-1, is almost equal to the earnings-maximizing size of Informal-1.

evidence of entry-barriers into the formal sector. Given the significantly lower earnings in the lower-paid informal sector, this would mean that being employed in this sector brings along considerable non-wage advantages that the formal sector cannot offer. However, we think that the informal sector should not have *more* (and we argue rather less) positive non-wage features than the formal sector. Whereas the informal sector offers more flexibility, the formal sector provides access to employment certainty, social security, medical insurance, pension funds etc. Hence, treating individuals as earnings maximizers should not significantly bias our results.[17]

## 4.4 Conclusion

In this paper we formulate an econometric model that allows for various sectors in the labor market, when sector affiliation of any particular individual is not necessarily observed. In addition, the model accounts for sample selection due to individuals' employment decision. The model further suggests a straightforward test for labor market segmentation.

We apply the model to study the structure of the urban labor market in Côte d'Ivoire. Our estimation results support the hypothesis that informal labor markets in developing countries are composed of two segments with a distinct wage equation in each of them. We further state that both informal sectors are considerable in size and make up 60 percent and 40 percent of informal employment, respectively. In addition, we show that one segment of the informal sector (the higher-paid informal sector) is superior to the other (the lower-paid informal sector) in terms of significantly higher earnings as well as higher returns to education and experience.

We also test whether the detected structure of the informal sector is a result of market segmentation that deters individuals from entering the formal sector, or a result of comparative advantage considerations of workers. Our results reject unlimited intersectoral mobility of workers and indicate that the lower-paid informal sector is largely the result of market segmentation whereas comparative

[17]However, there might be a difference for men and women, with the flexibility of the informal sector offering more advantages for women (usually being the once raising children) than for men.

advantage considerations seem to be the cause for the existence of the higher-paid informal sector. Hence, the informal sector comprises both individuals for whom the informal sector is a strategy of last resort to escape involuntary unemployment and individuals who are voluntarily employed in the informal sector. As a result, among the existing theoretical views on the structure of the informal labor market in developing economics, the one of Fields (2005) gets the largest empirical support.

For the theoretical modeling of labor markets in developing economies this means that there might exist cases in which neither solely competitive theories nor exclusively segmented labor market theories will provide an appropriate explanation of labor market interactions. Moreover, we might even rethink the general assumption of no entry-barriers into the informal sector, with entry-barriers to the higher-paid informal sector.

For the empirical literature our results clearly show that testing for labor market segmentation in developing economies can be misspecified by either ignoring the employment decision of individuals (e.g. Dickens and Lang, 1985; and Cunningham and Maloney, 2001) or by assuming away a possible latent structure of the labor market (e.g. Heckman and Sedlacek, 1985; Magnac, 1990). However, the later two papers address the interesting issue of specific entry-barriers, namely mobility costs, between the formal and informal sector (Magnac, 1991) and the issue of sector choice of utility-maximizing individuals (Heckman and Sedlacek, 1985), which we do not consider in this paper. It would be interesting to see the impact of a latent heterogenous informal sector on their models' estimation results. Last, our results demonstrate the importance to distinguish between male and female labor markets, which might show significant differences in structure and dynamics.

Our findings are particularly important for the design of policy measures which aim to reduce informality with low and unsecured earnings. Clearly, to talk about any specific policy measures, one needs to have at least a simple theoretical model that addresses the costs and benefits of decreasing the informal sector, which we do not provide in this paper. However, if we aim for policies with the objective to promote formal employment, we have to take into account that the informal sector consists of both individuals who would like to switch to a formal job and individuals who currently have no incentive of doing so. Policy recommendations for those two informal segments should be quite different. Although in both sectors of the informal labor market individuals face 'poor' earnings opportunities, it seems that individuals work in the higher-paid informal sector because they are poor(ly endowed) with necessary characteristics for the formal sector whereas individuals are poor because they involuntarily work in the lower-paid sector.

In the upper-tier informal sector, policies should address individuals' 'poor' endowments to improve their earnings possibilities in the formal sector. Moreover, this segment of the informal sector might also be partly 'responsible' for the high tax evasion in developing countries. Hence, measures to transform the higher-paid informal sector into the formal sector, i.e. to improve tax collection in this part of the labor market, might be enhanced.

With regard to individuals, who are involuntarily trapped in the informal sector, policy interventions have to counter entry-barriers into the formal sector. Moreover, workers found in this part of the informal market show especially low earnings. Hence, if the objective is to address the most disadvantaged first, the lower-paid informal sector should receive highest priority.

Last, before implementing any policies certain revealing mechanism that allow to determine whether any given individual belongs to one or another segment of the informal labor market need to be established. Even though no mixture model detects with certainty the affiliation of any given individual to any latent segment of the labor market our estimations results for wage functions in the different segments might already provide a guide for policy makers. For example, Table 4.4 reveals that young and uneducated males, living in Abidjan, mainly constitute the upper-tier informal sector, i.e. individuals who voluntarily work in the informal sector.[18]

[18]Note that the intercept in the higher-paid informal sector is higher than in the formal sector. Thus individuals with no or low endowments should earn more in the higher-paid informal sector than in the formal sector. Moreover, being a male and living in Abidjan yields higher returns in the higher-paid informal sector than in the formal sector.

# Appendix A

**STATA 8.0 Macro for a Triple Poverty Decomposition.**

```
#delimit;
set trace off;
cap program drop tripledecomposition;
program define tripledecomposition, rclass;
version 8.0;
syntax using [fweight aweight] [if], var1(varname numeric) var2(string)
pline1(string) pline2(string);

quietly {;
tempvar poor;
if ("‘if’" ="") keep ‘if’;
    gen ‘poor’=(‘var1’<‘pline1’);
    sum ‘poor’ [‘weight’ ‘exp’], meanonly; local prate111=r(mean);
    **poverty rate at mu1 and sigma1 and pline1;
    replace ‘poor’=(‘var1’<‘pline2’);
    sum ‘poor’ [‘weight’ ‘exp’], meanonly; local prate112=r(mean);
    **poverty rate at mu1 and sigma1 and pline2;
use ‘using’, clear;
if ("‘if’" ="") keep ‘if’;
    gen ‘poor’=(‘var2’<‘pline1’);
    sum ‘poor’ [‘weight’ ‘exp’], meanonly; local prate221=r(mean);
    **poverty rate at mu2 and sigma2 and pline1;
    replace ‘poor’=(‘var2’<‘pline2’);
    sum ‘poor’ [‘weight’ ‘exp’], meanonly; local prate222=r(mean);
```

```
    ** poverty rate at mu2 and sigma2 and pline2;
preserve;
    sum ‘var1’ [‘weight’ ‘exp’], meanonly; local mean11=r(mean);
    sum ‘var2’ [‘weight’ ‘exp’], meanonly; local mean22=r(mean);
    replace ‘var2’ = ‘var2’*‘mean11’/‘mean22’;
    gen ‘poor’ =(‘var2’<‘pline1’);
    sum ‘poor’ [‘weight’ ‘exp’], meanonly; local prate121=r(mean);
    **poverty rate at mu1 and sigma2 and pline1;
    replace ‘poor’ =(‘var2’<‘pline2’);
    sum ‘poor’ [‘weight’ ‘exp’], meanonly; local prate122=r(mean);
    **poverty rate at mu1 and sigma2 and pline2;
restore;
preserve;
    replace ‘var1’=‘var1’*‘mean22’/‘mean11’;
    gen ‘poor’=(‘var1’<‘pline1’);
    sum ‘poor’ [‘weight’ ‘exp’], meanonly; local prate211=r(mean);
    **poverty rate at mu2 and sigma1 and pline1;
    replace ‘poor’ =(‘var1’<‘pline2’);
    sum ‘poor’ [‘weight’ ‘exp’], meanonly; local prate212=r(mean);
    **poverty rate at mu2 and sigma1 and pline2;
restore;
    local changep =‘prate222’ - ‘prate111’;
    local growth1 =‘prate211’ - ‘prate111’;
    local growth2a =‘prate221’ - ‘prate121’;
    local growth2b =‘prate212’ - ‘prate112’;
    local growth2 =‘prate222’ - ‘prate122’;
    local redist1 =‘prate121’ - ‘prate111’;
    local redist2a =‘prate221’ - ‘prate211’;
    local redist2b =‘prate122’ - ‘prate112’;
    local redist2 =‘prate222’ - ‘prate212’;
    local povl1 = ‘prate112’ - ‘prate111’;
    local povl2a =‘prate212’ - ‘prate211’;
    local povl2b =‘prate122’ - ‘prate121’;
    local povl2 =‘prate222’ - ‘prate221’;
```

```
    local res = 'changep'- 'growth1'-'redist2a'-'povl2';
};
    disp in green "hline 80";
    disp in white " Growth and Inequality Poverty Decomposition";
    disp in green "hline 80";
    disp in green " Poverty Rate in Y.1" in yellow _col(32) %6.3f 'prate111';
    disp in green " Poverty Rate in Y.2" in yellow _col(32) %6.3f 'prate222';
    disp in green "hline 80";
    disp in green "Change in Poverty" in yellow _col(68) %6.3f 'changep';
    disp in green "hline 80";
    disp in green "Growth Component" in yellow _col(68) %6.3f
    ('growth1'+'growth1'+'growth2a'+'growth2b'+'growth2'+'growth2')/6;
    disp in green "Redistribution Component" in yellow _col(68) %6.3f
    ('redist1'+'redist1'+'redist2a'+'redist2b'+'redist2'+'redist2')/6;
    disp in green "Poverty Line Component" in yellow _col(68) %6.3f
    ('povl1'+'povl1'+'povl2a'+'povl2b'+'povl2'+'povl2')/6;
    disp in green "Residual" in yellow
    _col(68) %6.3f 'res';
    disp in green "hline 80";
end;
```

# Appendix B

**Component Density of the Error Term.**

Consider a component density $f(u_i|u_{is} > -\mathbf{z}_i\gamma, \theta_j)$. Using Bayes rule (for simplicity of notation we suppress conditioning on $y_i \in \mathscr{Y}_j$) we get

$$f(u_i|u_{is} > -\mathbf{z}_i\gamma, \theta_j) = \frac{P(u_{is} > -\mathbf{z}_i\gamma|u_i, \theta_j) f(u_i|\theta_j)}{P(u_{is} > -\mathbf{z}_i\gamma)}.$$

Since the joint distribution of $(u_i, u_{is})$ is bivariate normal, the conditional density $f(u_{is}|u_i, \theta_j)$ follows $N(\frac{\rho_j}{\sigma_j}u_i, 1-\rho_j^2)$ and the marginal density $f(u_i|\theta_j) \sim N(0, \sigma_j^2)$. Thus

$$\begin{aligned} f(u_i|u_{is} > -\mathbf{z}_i\gamma, \theta_j) &= P\left(\frac{u_{is} - \mathbf{z}_i\gamma - \rho_j\sigma_j^{-1}u_i}{\sqrt{1-\rho_j^2}} > \frac{-\mathbf{z}_i\gamma - \rho_j\sigma_j^{-1}u_i}{\sqrt{1-\rho_j^2}}\right) \frac{f(u_i|\theta_j)}{P(u_{is} > -\mathbf{z}_i\gamma)} \\ &= \Phi\left(\frac{\mathbf{z}_i\gamma + \rho_j\sigma_j^{-1}\left[\ln y_i - \mathbf{x}_i\beta_j\right]}{\sqrt{1-\rho_j^2}}\right) \frac{1}{\sigma_j}\varphi\left(\frac{\ln y_i - \mathbf{x}_i\beta_j}{\sigma_j}\right) \frac{1}{\Phi(\mathbf{z}_i\gamma)}, \end{aligned}$$

where $\theta_j = \{\beta_j, \sigma_j, \rho_j\}$ and $\varphi$ and $\Phi$ are the probability density and distribution functions of the standard normal distribution.

**Proof of Proposition 1.**

Consider the component density of (4.7)

$$h_j(y'|\mu_j, \sigma_j, \rho_j) = \frac{\varphi\left(\sigma_j^{-1}\left[y' - \mu_j\right]\right)}{\sigma_j\Phi(a)} \Phi\left(\frac{a + \rho_j\sigma_j^{-1}\left[y' - \mu_j\right]}{\sqrt{1-\rho_j^2}}\right),$$

where we define $\mu_j = \mathbf{x}\boldsymbol{\beta}_j$, $a = \mathbf{z}\gamma$ and $y' = \ln y$. Bilateral Laplace transform of this density is

$$\begin{aligned}
\phi_j[h(y')](t) &= \int_{-\infty}^{+\infty} e^{-ty} \frac{\varphi\left(\sigma_j^{-1}\left[y' - \mu_j\right]\right)}{\sigma_j \Phi(a)} \Phi\left(\frac{a + \rho_j \sigma_j^{-1}\left[y' - \mu_j\right]}{\sqrt{1-\rho_j^2}}\right) dy' \\
&= \frac{1}{\Phi(a)} \int_{-\infty}^{+\infty} e^{-t\left(\sigma_j z + \mu_j\right)} \frac{e^{-\frac{1}{2}z^2}}{\sqrt{2\pi}} \Phi\left(\frac{a + \rho_j z}{\sqrt{1-\rho_j^2}}\right) dz \\
&= \frac{e^{-t\mu_j}}{\Phi(a)} \int_{-\infty}^{+\infty} \frac{e^{-t\sigma_j z - \frac{1}{2}z^2}}{\sqrt{2\pi}} \Phi\left(\frac{a + \rho_j z}{\sqrt{1-\rho_j^2}}\right) dz \\
&= \frac{e^{\frac{1}{2}t^2\sigma_j^2 - t\mu_j}}{\Phi(a)} \int_{-\infty}^{+\infty} \frac{e^{-\frac{1}{2}\left(z + t\sigma_j\right)^2}}{\sqrt{2\pi}} \Phi\left(\frac{a + \rho_j z}{\sqrt{1-\rho_j^2}}\right) dz \\
&= \frac{e^{\frac{1}{2}t^2\sigma_j^2 - t\mu_j}}{\Phi(a)} \int_{-\infty}^{+\infty} \varphi\left(z + t\sigma_j\right) \Phi\left(\frac{a + \rho_j z}{\sqrt{1-\rho_j^2}}\right) dz.
\end{aligned}$$

Applying integration by parts to

$$\phi_j(t) = \frac{e^{\frac{1}{2}t^2\sigma_j^2 - t\mu_j}}{\Phi(a)} \int_{-\infty}^{+\infty} \varphi\left(z + t\sigma_j\right) \Phi\left(\frac{a + \rho_j z}{\sqrt{1-\rho_j^2}}\right) dz$$

we get:

$$\begin{aligned}
\phi_j(t) &\overset{\rho_j \neq 0}{=} \frac{e^{\frac{1}{2}t^2\sigma_j^2 - t\mu_j}}{\Phi(a)} \left[ \Phi\left(\frac{a + \rho_j z}{\sqrt{1-\rho_j^2}}\right) \Phi\left(z + t\sigma_j\right) \Bigg|_{-\infty}^{+\infty} \right. \\
&\qquad \left. - \frac{\rho_j}{\sqrt{1-\rho_j^2}} \int_{-\infty}^{+\infty} \varphi\left(\frac{a + \rho_j z}{\sqrt{1-\rho_j^2}}\right) \Phi\left(z + t\sigma_j\right) dz \right] \\
&= \frac{e^{\frac{1}{2}t^2\sigma_j^2 - t\mu_j}}{\Phi(a)} \left[ 1 - \frac{\rho_j}{\sqrt{1-\rho_j^2}} \int_{-\infty}^{+\infty} \varphi\left(\frac{a + \rho_j z}{\sqrt{1-\rho_j^2}}\right) \Phi\left(z + t\sigma_j\right) dz \right].
\end{aligned}$$

Also notice that for $\rho_j = 0$ the transform reduces to that of the normal distribution.

Let $S_j$ denote the domain of definition of $\phi_j(t)$. First, for any $l, j$ we get $S_j \subseteq S_l$. This fulfills the first requirement of Theorem 2 in Teicher (1963). Second, we seek for a limiting behavior of $\phi_l(t)/\phi_j(t)$ once $t \to t_*$ for some $t_* \in \bar{S}_j$. Consider:

$$\lim_{t\to+\infty}\frac{\phi_l(t)}{\phi_j(t)} = \lim_{t\to+\infty}\frac{e^{\frac{1}{2}t^2\sigma_l^2-t\mu_l}}{e^{\frac{1}{2}t^2\sigma_j^2-t\mu_j}}\lim_{t\to+\infty}\frac{1-\frac{\rho_l}{\sqrt{1-\rho_l^2}}\int_{-\infty}^{+\infty}\varphi\left(\frac{a+\rho_l z}{\sqrt{1-\rho_l^2}}\right)\Phi\left(z+t\sigma_l\right)dz}{1-\frac{\rho_j}{\sqrt{1-\rho_j^2}}\int_{-\infty}^{+\infty}\varphi\left(\frac{a+\rho_j z}{\sqrt{1-\rho_j^2}}\right)\Phi\left(z+t\sigma_j\right)dz}.$$

Applying l'Hospital's rule to the second limit, we get

$$\lim_{t\to+\infty}\frac{\phi_l(t)}{\phi_j(t)} = \lim_{t\to+\infty} e^{\frac{1}{2}t^2(\sigma_l^2-\sigma_j^2)-t(\mu_l-\mu_j)}$$
$$\times\lim_{t\to+\infty}\frac{\int_{-\infty}^{+\infty}\varphi\left(\frac{a+\rho_l z}{\sqrt{1-\rho_l^2}}\right)\varphi\left(z+t\sigma_l\right)dz}{\int_{-\infty}^{+\infty}\varphi\left(\frac{a+\rho_j z}{\sqrt{1-\rho_j^2}}\right)\varphi\left(z+t\sigma_j\right)dz}\left[\frac{\rho_l\sigma_l\sqrt{1-\rho_j^2}}{\rho_j\sigma_j\sqrt{1-\rho_l^2}}\right].$$

For the integral

$$\int_{-\infty}^{+\infty}\varphi\left(\frac{a+\rho_j z}{\sqrt{1-\rho_j^2}}\right)\varphi\left(z+t\sigma_j\right)dz$$

by factorization of the Gaussian kernel for $z$ it can be shown that

$$\begin{aligned}
&\int_{-\infty}^{+\infty}\varphi\left(\frac{a+\rho_j z}{\sqrt{1-\rho_j^2}}\right)\varphi\left(z+t\sigma_j\right)dz\\
&= \int_{-\infty}^{+\infty}\frac{1}{\sqrt{2\pi}}\exp\left\{-\frac{1}{2}\frac{\left(a+\rho_j z\right)^2}{1-\rho_j^2}\right\}\frac{1}{\sqrt{2\pi}}\exp\left\{-\frac{1}{2}\left(z+t\sigma_j\right)^2\right\}dz\\
&= \int_{-\infty}^{+\infty}\frac{1}{2\pi}\exp\left\{-\frac{1}{2}\left[\left\{\frac{\left(a+\rho_j z\right)^2}{1-\rho_j^2}\right\}+\left\{\left(z+t\sigma_j\right)^2\right\}\right]\right\}dz\\
&= \int_{-\infty}^{+\infty}\frac{1}{2\pi}\exp\left\{-\frac{1}{2}\left[\left\{\left(a-t\sigma_j\rho_j\right)^2\right\}+\left\{\frac{\left(z+\left[a\rho_j+t\sigma_j\left(1-\rho_j^2\right)\right]\right)^2}{1-\rho_j^2}\right\}\right]\right\}dz
\end{aligned}$$

$$= \int_{-\infty}^{+\infty} \varphi\left(a - t\sigma_j\rho_j\right) \varphi\left(\frac{z + \left[a\rho_j + t\sigma_j\left(1-\rho_j^2\right)\right]}{\sqrt{1-\rho_j^2}}\right) dz$$

$$= \varphi\left(a - t\sigma_j\rho_j\right)\sqrt{1-\rho_j^2}\underbrace{\int_{-\infty}^{+\infty} \frac{1}{\sqrt{1-\rho_j^2}} \varphi\left(\frac{z + \left[a\rho_j + t\sigma_j\left(1-\rho_j^2\right)\right]}{\sqrt{1-\rho_j^2}}\right) dz}_{=1}$$

$$= \varphi\left(a - t\sigma_j\rho_j\right)\sqrt{1-\rho_j^2}.$$

With this result the limit of the ratio of the two transforms becomes

$$\lim_{t\to+\infty} \frac{\phi_l(t)}{\phi_j(t)}$$

$$= \lim_{t\to+\infty} e^{\frac{1}{2}t^2\left(\sigma_l^2-\sigma_j^2\right)-t\left(\mu_l-\mu_j\right)} \lim_{t\to+\infty} \frac{\varphi\left(a-t\sigma_l\rho_l\right)}{\varphi\left(a-t\sigma_j\rho_j\right)} \left[\frac{\rho_l\sigma_l}{\rho_j\sigma_j}\right]$$

$$= \lim_{t\to+\infty} e^{\frac{1}{2}t^2\left(\sigma_l^2-\sigma_j^2\right)-t\left(\mu_l-\mu_j\right)} \lim_{t\to+\infty} e^{-\frac{1}{2}t^2\left(\sigma_l^2\rho_l^2-\sigma_j^2\rho_j^2\right)+ta\left(\sigma_l\rho_l-\sigma_j\rho_j\right)} \left[\frac{\rho_l\sigma_l}{\rho_j\sigma_j}\right]$$

$$= \lim_{t\to+\infty} e^{\frac{1}{2}t^2\left(\sigma_l^2\left[1-\rho_l^2\right]-\sigma_j^2\left[1-\rho_j^2\right]\right)-t\left(\left[\mu_l-\mu_j\right]-a\left[\sigma_l\rho_l-\sigma_j\rho_j\right]\right)} \left[\frac{\rho_l\sigma_l}{\rho_j\sigma_j}\right]$$

Repeating the ordering argument of Teicher (1963) we see that the general class of mixtures in (4.7) is not identifiable because there is no lexicographic order $h_j(y) \prec_{\sigma,\rho} h_l(y)$ that can insure that the leading term in the exponent will always converge to zero as $t_* \to +\infty$. However, restricting the attention to a sub-class, in which $\rho_l = \rho_j \; \forall l, j \in [1, J]$ we obtain the claimed result. For any $l, j \in [1, J]$ let $\rho_l = \rho_j$ and order the subfamily lexicographically so that $h_j\left(y; \mu_j, \sigma_j, \rho\right) \prec h_j\left(y; \mu_l, \sigma_l, \rho\right)$ if $\sigma_l < \sigma_j$ and $\mu_l > \mu_j$ when $\sigma_l = \sigma_j$. Then for $t_* = +\infty$, $t_* \in \overline{S}_j$ we get

$$\lim_{t\to t_*} \phi_l(t)/\phi_j(t) = 0,$$

which fulfills the second and the last requirement of Theorem 2 in Teicher (1963). Since the sufficient condition of Teicher (1963) applies, the sub-class of finite mixtures (4.7) with common $\rho$ is identifiable. ∎

**Remark 1.**

From the proof above immediately follows that allowing for a sector-specific selection rule (i.e., letting $a$ be $a_j = \mathbf{z}\gamma_j$) leads to an unidentifiable model, since the limit of ratio writes

$$\lim_{t\to+\infty}\frac{\phi_l(t)}{\phi_j(t)}$$
$$= \lim_{t\to+\infty} e^{\frac{1}{2}t^2\left(\sigma_l^2\left[1-\rho_l^2\right]-\sigma_j^2\left[1-\rho_j^2\right]\right)-t\left(\left[\mu_l-\mu_j\right]-\left[a_l\sigma_l\rho_l-a_j\sigma_j\rho_j\right]\right)}\frac{\rho_l\sigma_l\Phi(a_j)}{\rho_j\sigma_j\Phi(a_j)}e^{-\frac{1}{2}(a_l^2-a_j^2)}$$

and even within the considered sub-class of $\rho_l = \rho_j = \rho$ there is no ordering over $\{\mu\}$ which will insure that this limit is zero once $\sigma_l = \sigma_j$.

**Estimation of the Distribution in (4.9).**

Once individuals are free to enter the sector that pays them, conditional on their characteristics, the highest expected wage, the distribution of agents across sectors becomes

$$P\left(y\in\mathscr{Y}_j\right) = P\left(E\left[\ln y^j|y_s>0;\mathbf{x}\right] = \max_{l,l\neq j}\left\{E\left[\ln y^l|y_s>0;\mathbf{x}\right]\right\}\right).$$

Define the indicator function $I(y_i^j)$ such that $I(y_i^j) = 1$ if $E\left[\ln y_i^j|y_{is}>0;\mathbf{x}_i\right] = \max_{l,l\neq j}\left\{E\left[\ln y_i^l|y_{is}>0;\mathbf{x}_i\right]\right\}$ and $I(y_i^j) = 0$ otherwise. Then the above probability distribution can be estimated by

$$P\left(y\in\mathscr{Y}_j\right) = n^{-1}\sum_{i=1}^{n} I(y_i^j),$$

where the estimated sector-specific expected log-wage for every individual is given by

$$E\left[\ln y_i^j|y_{is}>0,\mathbf{x}_i\right] = \mathbf{x}_i\hat{\beta}_j + \hat{\rho}\hat{\sigma}_j\frac{\varphi(-\mathbf{z}_i\hat{\gamma})}{1-\Phi(-\mathbf{z}_i\hat{\gamma})}.$$

# Bibliography


AFD (2003). Perspectives économiques et financières des pays de la zone franc. *Report*, Département de La Recherche, AFD, Paris.

ANDREWS, D. (1988). Chi-Square Diagnostic Tests for Econometric Models. *Econometrica* 56(6): 1419-1453.

ARROW, K. (1958). The Measurement of Price Changes. In: *The Relationship of Prices to Economic Stability and Growth*, U.S. Congress, Washington D.C.: U.S. Government Printing Office.

AZAM, J.-P. (2004). Poverty and Growth in the WAEMU after the 1994 Devaluation. *UNU/WIDER Research Paper* 2004/19, United Nations University, WIDER, Helsinki.

BANERJEE, A., BARDHAN, P., BASU, K. AND KANBUR R. (2005). Theory versus Empirics in Development Economics: A Symposium. *bu economics working paper* 28, Boston University, Boston.

BASU, A. (1997). *Analytical Development Economics*, Cambridge : MIT Press

BAULCH, B. AND J. HODDINOTT (2000). Economic mobility and poverty dynamics in developing countries. *Journal of Development Studies* 36(6): 1-24.

BOSKIN, M., DULBERGER, E., GORDON, R., GRILICHES, Z. AND D. JORGENSON (1997). The CPI Commission: Findings and Recommendations. *Amercian Economic Review* 87(2): 78-83.

BOURGUIGNON, F. (2003). The growth elasticity of poverty reduction: explaining heterogeneity across countries and time periods. In: Eicher, T. and S. Turnovsky (eds.), *Growth and Inequality*, Boston: MIT Press.

BRYK, A.S. AND S.W. RAUDENBUSH (1992). *Hierarchical Linear Models: Applications and Data Analysis*, Newbury Park: Sage Publications.

CALVO, C. AND S. DERCON (2005). Measuring Individual Vulnerability. *Discussion Paper* 229, University of Oxford, Oxford.

CARTER, M. (1997). Environment, Technology, and the Social Articulation of Risk in West African Agriculture. *Economic Development and Cultural Change* 45(3): 557-590.

CHAUDHURI, S. (2002). Empirical methods for assessing household vulnerability to poverty. Mimeo, Columbia University, New York.

CHAUDHURI, S., JALAN, J. AND A. SURYAHADI (2002). Assessing Household Vulnerability to Poverty from Cross-sectional Data: A Methodology and Estimates from Indonesia. *Discussion Paper* 0102-52, Columbia University, New York.

CHAUDHURI, S. (2003). Assessing vulnerability to poverty: concepts, empirical methods and illustrative examples. Mimeo, Columbia University, New York.

CORD, L., LOPEZ, H. AND J. PAGE (2003). When I use a word. Mimeo, World Bank, Washington D.C.

CRAWFORD, I. AND Z. SMITH (2002). Distributional aspects of inflation. Mimeo, The Institute for Fiscal Studies, London.

CUNNINGHAM, W. AND W.F. MALONEY (2001). Heterogeneity in the Mexican Micro-Enterprise Sector: An Application of Factor and Cluster Analysis. *Economic Development and Cultural Change* 5: 131-156.

DATT, G. AND M. RAVALLION (1992). Growth and redistribution components of changes in poverty measures. A decomposition with applications to

Brazil and India in the 1980s. *Journal of Development Economics* 38(2): 275-295.

DAVIDSON, R. AND J.Y. DUCLOS (2000). Statistical Inference for Stochastic Dominance and for the Measurement of Poverty and Inequality. *Econometrica* 68(6): 1435-1465.

DEATON, A. (1997) *The Analysis of Household Surveys*, Baltimore: John Hopkins University Press.

DEATON, A. (1998). Getting Prices Right: What should be done? *Journal of Economic Perspectives* 12(1): 37-46.

DEATON, A. (2003a). Prices and Poverty in India 1987-2000. *Economic and Political Weekly*, January 25: 362-368.

DEATON, A. (2003b). Measuring poverty in a growing world (or measuring growth in a poor world). *NBER Working Paper* 9822, NBER, Cambridge MA.

DEATON, A. AND J. DRÈZE (2002). Poverty and inequality in India, a reexamination. *Economic and Political Weekly*, September 7: 3729-3748.

DEATON, A. AND C. PAXSON (1998). Economies of Scale, Household Size, and the Demand for Food. *Journal of Political Economy* 106(5): 897-930.

DEATON, A. AND S. ZAIDI (2002). *Guidelines for Constructing Consumption Aggregates for Welfare Analysis*, World Bank, Washington D.C.

DERCON, S. AND P. KRISHNAN (2000). Vulnerability, seasonality and poverty in Ethiopia. *Journal of Development Studies* 36(6): 25-53.

DICKENS, W.T. AND K. LANG (1985). A Test of Dual Labor Market Theory. *American Economic Review* 75(4): 792-805.

DOLLAR, D. AND A. KRAY (2002). Growth is good for the poor. *Journal of Economic Growth* 7(3): 195-225.

DORWAD, A., KYDD, J., MORRISON, J. AND I. UREY (2004). A Policy Agenda for Pro-Poor Agricultural Growth. *World Development* 32(1): 73-89.

EEC (1985). On Specific Community Action to Combat Poverty. Council Decision of 19 December 1984. *Official Journal of the EEC* 2(24).

ELBERS, C., GUNNING, J.W. AND B. KINSEY (2003). Growth and Risk: Methodology and Micro Evidence. *Tinbergen Institute Discussion Paper* TI 2003-068/2, Tinbergen Institute, Tinbergen.

ENGEL, E. (1895). Die Lebenskosten Belgischer Arbeiter-Familien. Früher und Jetzt. *International Statistical Bulletin* 9: 1-74.

FIELDS, G.S. (1975). Rural-urban Migration, Urban Unemployment and Underemployment, and Job-search Activity in LDCs. *Journal of Development Economics* 2(2): 165-87.

FIELDS, G.S. (1990). Labour Market Modelling and the Urban Informal Sector: Theory and Evidence. In: Thurnham, D., Salome, B. and A. Schwarz (eds.), *The Informal Sector Revisited*, OECD, Paris.

FIELDS, G.S. (2005). A Guide to Multisector Labor Market Models. *Paper* for the World Bank Labor Market Conference, World Bank, Washington D.C.

FIELDS, G.S., CICHELLO, P.L., FREIJE, S., MENENDEZ, M. AND D. NEWHOUSE (2005). Household Income Dynamics: A Four Country Story. *Journal of Development Studies* 40(2): 30-54.

FILMER, D. AND L.H. PRITCHETT (2001). Estimating Wealth Effects without Expenditure Data - or Tears: An Application to Educational Enrollments in States of India. *Demography* 38(1): 115-132.

FOFACK, H., MONGA, C. AND H. TULUY (2001). Household Welfare and Poverty Dynamics in Burkina Faso: Empirical Evidence from Household Surveys. *World Bank Policy Research Working Paper* 2590, World Bank, Washington D.C.

FOSTER, J., GREER, J. AND E. THORBECKE (1984). A class of decomposable poverty measures. *Econometrica* 52(3): 761-5.

GENICOT, G. AND D. RAY (2003). Endogenous Group Formation in Risk-Sharing Arrangements. *Review of Economic Studies* 70(1): 87-113.

GERTLER, P. AND J. GRUBER (2002). Insuring Consumption Against Illness. *American Economic Review* 92(1): 55-70.

GINDLING, T. (1991). Labor Market Segmentation and the Determination of Wages in the Public, Private-Formal and Informal Sectors in San-Jose, Costa-Rica. *Economic Development and Cultural Change* 39(3): 585-603.

GLEWWE, P. AND G. HALL. (1998). Are some groups more vulnerable to macroeconomic shocks than others. Hypothesis tests based on panel data from Peru. *Journal of Development Economics* 56(1): 181-206.

GOLDSTEIN, H. (1999). *Multilevel Statistical Models*, London: Arnold.

GORAD, S. (2003). What is Multi-Level for? *British Journal of Educational Studies* 51(1): 46-63.

GRIMM, M. AND I. GÜNTHER (2004). How to achieve pro-poor growth in a poor economy. The case of Burkina Faso. *Report* for the 'Operationalizing Pro-Poor-Growth'-Project by the Worldbank, DFID, AFD, GTZ, and KFW, University of Göttingen, Göttingen.

GRIMM, M. (2006). Mortality and Survivors' Consumption. *DIW Discussion Paper* 611, German Institute for Economic Research, Berlin.

GROSSE, M., HARTTGEN, K. AND S. KLASEN (2006). Measuring Pro-Poor Progress towards the Non-Income Millennium Development Goals. *IAI Discussion Paper* 144, Ibero-America Institute for Economic Research, Göttingen.

GUÉNARD, C. (1998). Evolution de la structure des prix et impact sur les inégalités de niveau de vie à Antananarivo de 1990 a 1997. *Working Paper* DT/98/05, DIAL, Paris.

HADDAD, L., RUEL, M.T. AND J.L. GARRETT (1999). Are urban poverty and undernutrition growing? Some newly assembled evidence. *World Development* 27(11): 1891-1904.

HARRIS, J.R. AND M.P. TODARO (1970). Migration, unemployment and development: A two-sector analysis. *American Economic Review* 60(1): 126-142.

HART, K. (1973). Informal Income Opportunities and Urban Employment in Ghana. *Journal of Modern African Studies* 11(2): 61-89.

HECKMAN, J. (1979). Sample Selection Bias as a Specification Error. *Econometrica* 47(1): 153-161.

HECKMAN, J. AND V. HOTZ (1986). An Investigation of the Labor Market Earnings of Panamanian Males. *Journal of Human Resources* 21(4): 507-542.

HECKMAN, J. AND G. SEDLACEK (1985). Heterogeneity, Aggregation and Market Wage Functions: An Empirical Model of Self-Selection in the Labor Market. *Journal of Political Economy* 93(6): 1077-1125.

HOBIJN, B. AND D. LAGAKOS (2003). Inflation Inequality in the United States. *Staff Report* 173, Federal Reserve Bank of New York, New York.

HODDINOTT, J. AND A. QUISUMBING (2003). Methods for Microeconometric Risk and Vulnerability Assessments. *Social Protection Discussion Paper* 0324, World Bank, Washington D.C.

HOX, J. (2002). *Multilevel Analysis - Techniques and Applications*, Mahwah: Lawrence Erlbaum Associates.

ILO (1972). Employment, incomes and equality: A strategy for increasing productive employment in Kenya. *Report*, ILO, Geneva.

IMF (2003). Burkina Faso. *IMF Country Report* 03/197, International Monetary Fund, Washington D.C.

IMF (2005). Burkina Faso. *IMF Country Report* 05/358, International Monetary Fund, Washington D.C.

INSD (1998). Analyse des résultats de l'enquête sur les dépenses des ménages de Ouagadougou. *Report*, Institut National de la Statistique et de la Démographie, Ouagadougou.

INSD (2003). Burkina Faso: La pauvreté en 2003. *Report*, Institut National de la Statistique et de la Démographie, Ouagadougou.

JÄNTTI, M. AND S. DANZIGER (2000). Income Poverty in Advanced Countries. In: Atkinson, B. and F. Bourguignon (eds.), *Handbook of Income Distribution*, Amsterdam: North-Holland.

JALAN, J. AND M. RAVALLION (1999). Are the poor less well insured? Evidence on vulnerability to income risk in rural China. *Journal of Development Economics* 58(1): 61-81.

JOLLIFFE, D. (2001). Measuring absolute and relative poverty: The sensitivity of estimated household consumption to survey design. *Journal of Economic and Social Measurement* 27(1/2): 1-23.

KAKWANI, N. AND E. PERNIA (2000). What is Pro-Poor Growth? *Asian Development Review* 18(1): 1-16.

KANBUR, R. AND L. SQUIRE (2001). The Evolution of Thinking About Poverty: Exploring the Interactions. In: Meier G. and J. Stiglitz (eds.), *Frontiers of Development Economics: The Future in Perspective*, Oxford: Oxford University Press.

KILPATRICK, R.W. (1973). The Income Elasticity of the Poverty Line. *The Review of Economics and Statistics* 55(3): 327-332.

KLASEN, S. (1994). Growth and Well-Being: Introducing Distribution-Weighted Growth Rates to Reassess Postwar US Economic Performance. *Review of Income and Wealth* 40(3): 251-272.

KLASEN, S. (2000). Measuring Poverty and Deprivation in South Africa. *Review of Income and Wealth* 46(1): 33-58.

KLASEN, S. (2004). In Search of the Holy Grail. How to Achieve Pro Poor Growth. In: Stern, N. and B. Tungodden (eds.), *Towards Pro Poor Policies. Proceedings of the Annual Bank Conference on Development Economics (ABCDE) Europe Conference*, World Bank, Washington D.C.

KLASEN, S. (2006). Pro-Poor Growth and Gender Inequality.*IAI Discussion Paper* 151, Ibero-America Institute for Economic Research, Göttingen.

KLASEN, S. AND M. MISSELHORN (2006). Determinants of the Growth Semi-Elasticity of Poverty Reduction. Mimeo, University of Göttingen, Göttingen.

KOCHAR, A. (1995). Explaining Household Vulnerability to Idiosyncratic Income Shocks. *The American Economic Review* 85(2): 159-164.

KRAAY, A. (2003). When is Growth Pro-Poor? Evidence from a Panel of Countries. Mimeo, World Bank, Washington D.C.

KUZNETS, S. (1966). *Modern economic growth*. London: Yale University Press.

LACHAUD, J.P. (2003). Pauvreté et inégalité au Burkina Faso: Profil et dynamique. *Report*, UNDP, Ouagadougou.

LANJOUW, J.O. AND P. LANJOUW (2001). How to compare apples and oranges: Poverty measurement based on different definition of consumption. *Review of Income and Wealth* 47(1): 25-42.

LANJOUW, J.O. (1998). *Demystifying Poverty Lines*. New York: Poverty Elimination Programme, UNDP.

LEBOW, D. AND J. RUDD (2003). Measurement Error in the Consumer Price Index: Where Do we stand? *Journal of Economic Literature* 41(1): 159-201.

LEE, L.F. (1983). Generalized Econometric Models with Selectivity. *Econometrica* 51(2): 507-512.

LEMIEUX, T. (2006). Increasing Residual Wage Inequality. Composition Effects, Noisy Data, or Rising Demand for Skill? *American Economic Review* 96(3): 461-498.

LEWIS, W.A. (1954). Economic Development with Unlimited Supplies of Labour. *Manchester School* 28: 139-91.

LEY, E. (2005). Whose inflation? A characterization of the CPI plutocratic gap. *Oxford Economic Papers* 57: 634-646.

LIGON, E. AND S. SCHECHTER (2003). Measuring vulnerability. *Economic Journal* 113(486): C95-C102.

LIGON, E. AND S. SCHECHTER (2004). Evaluating Different Approaches to Estimating Vulnerability. *Social Protection Discussion Paper Series* 0410, World Bank, Washington D.C.

LINDSAY, B. AND K. ROEDER (1992). Residual Diagnostics for Mixture Models. *Journal of the American Statistical Association* 87(419): 785-794.

LITTLE, R. (1985). A Note about Models for Selectivity Bias. *Econometrica* 53(6): 1469-1474.

LIVINGSTONE, I. (1971). A Reassessment of Kenya's Rural and Urban Informal Sector. *World Development* 19(6): 651-70.

LOPEZ, H. (2003). Pro growth, pro poor: Is there a trade off?. Mimeo, World Bank, Washington D.C.

LUTTMER, E.F.P. (2000). Inequality and Poverty Dynamics in Transition Economies. Disentangling Real Events from Noisy Data. Mimeo, World Bank, Washington D.C.

MADALLA, G.S. (1977). *Econometrics*, Tokyo: McGraw-Hill.

MAGNAC, T. (1991). Segmented or Competitive Labor Markets. *Econometrica* 59(1): 165-187.

MALONEY, W.F. (2004). Informality Revisited. *World Development* 32(7): 1159-1178.

MAROUANI, M. AND M. RAFFINOT (2004). Perspectives on growth and poverty reduction in Mali. *Working Paper* DT/2004/05, DIAL, Paris.

MASON, W.M., WONG, G.M. AND B. ENTWISTLE (1983). Contextual analysis through the multilevel linear model. In: Leinhardt, S. (ed.), *Sociological Methodology*, San Francisco: Jossey-Bass.

MAAS, C.J.M. AND J. HOX (2004). Robustness issues in multilevel regression analysis, *Statistica Neerlandica*, 58(2): 127-137.

MAZUMDAR, D. (1976). The Urban Informal Sector. *World Development* 4(8): 655-79.

MCCULLOCH, N. AND B. BAULCH (2000). Tracking pro-poor growth. *ID21 Insights* 31, Institute of Development Studies, Sussex University, Sussex.

MILLS, B., NINNO, C. AND H. RAJEMISON (2003). Commune Shocks, Household Assets and Economic Wellbeing in Madagascar. Mimeo, World Bank, Washington D.C.

MINISTÈRE DE L'ECONOMIE ET DES FINANCES (1997). Une maquette macroéconomique pour gérer l'économie du Burkina Faso. *Report*, Ministère de l'Economie et des Finances, Ouagadougou.

MORDUCH, J. (1994). Poverty and Vulnerability. *The American Economic Review* 84(2): 221-225.

MORDUCH, J. (2005). Consumption smoothing across space: Testing theories of risk-sharing in the ICRISAT study region of South India. In: Dercon, S. (ed.) *Insurance against Poverty*, Oxford: Oxford University Press.

MURPHY, K. AND R. TOPEL (1985). Estimation and Inference in Two Step Econometric Models. *Journal of Business and Economics Statistics* 3(4): 370-379.

NARAYAN, D., PATEL, R., SCHAFFT, K., RADEMACHER, A. AND S. KOCH-SCHULTE (2000). *Voices of the poor: can anyone hear us?*, New York: Oxford University Press.

NEWBERY, D.M. (1995). The distributional impact of price changes in Hungary and the UK. *Economic Journal* 105(431): 847-863.

NICHOLSON, J.L. (1975). Whose cost of living? *Journal of the Royal Statistical Society*, Series A 138(4): 540-542.

OLSEN, R. (1980). A Least Squares Correction for Selectivity Bias. *Econometrica* 48(7): 1815-1820.

ORWELL, G. (1949). *Nineteen Eighty-Four*, London: Secker and Warburg.

PAXON, C.H. (1992). Using Weather Variability to Estimate the Response of Savings to Transitory Income in Thailand. *The American Economic Review* 82(1): 15-33.

PRAIS, S.J. (1959). Whose cost of living? *Review of Economic Studies* 26(2): 126-134.

PRITCHETT, L., SURYAHADI, A. AND S. SUMARTO (2000a). The evolution of poverty during the crisis in Indonesia, 1996 to 1999. *SMERU Working Paper*, World Bank, Washington D.C.

PRITCHETT, L., SURYAHADI, A. AND S. SUMARTO (2000b). Quantifying Vulnerability to Poverty: A Proposed Measure, with Application to Indonesia. *SMERU Working Paper*, World Bank, Washington D.C.

RAM, T. (2006). Growth Elasticity of Poverty: Alternative Estimates and a Note of Caution. *Kyklos* 59(4): 601-610.

RAVALLION, M. (2001). Growth, Inequality and Poverty: Looking Beyond Averages. *World Development* 29(11): 1787-1802.

RAVALLION, M. (2004). Pro-Poor Growth: A Primer. *Policy Research Working Paper* 3242, World Bank, Washington D.C.

RAVALLION, M. AND S. CHEN (1997). What can new survey data tell us about recent changes in distribution and poverty?. *World Bank Economic Review* 11(2): 357-382.

RAVALLION, M. AND G. DATT (1999). When is growth pro-poor? Evidence from the Diverse Experience of India's States. *Policy Research Working Paper* 2263, World Bank, Washington D.C.

RAVALLION, M. AND S. CHEN (2003). Measuring Pro-Poor Growth. *Economics Letters* 78(1): 93-99.

RAY, D. (1998). *Development Economics*, Princeton: Princeton University Press.

REARDON, T. AND P. MATLON (1989). Seasonal food insecurity and vulnerability in drought-affected regions in Burkina Faso. In: Sahn, D.E. (ed.), *Seasonal variability in third world agriculture. The consequences for food security*, Baltimore: Johns Hopkins University Press.

REDDY, S.G. AND T.W. POGGE (2005). How NOT to count the poor. Mimeo, Department of Economics, Columbia University, New York.

ROSENZWEIG, M. (1998). Labor Markets in Low Income Countries. In: Chenery H. and T.N. Srinivasan (eds.), *Handbook of Development Economics, Volume 1*, Amsterdam: North Holland.

SACHS, J. (2005). *The End of Poverty: Economic Possibilities for Our Time*, New York: Penguin Press.

SAHN, D.E. AND D. STIEFEL (2003). Exploring Alternative Measures of Welfare in the Absense of Expenditure Data. *Review of Income and Wealth* 49(4): 463-489.

SCOTT, C. AND B. AMENUVEGBE (1990). Effect of recall duration on reporting of household expenditures. Mimeo, World Bank, Washington D.C.

SEN, A. (1976). Poverty: An Ordinal Approach to Measurement. *Econometrica* 44(2): 219-231.

SEN, A. (1981). *Poverty and Famines - An Essay on Entitlement and Deprivation*, Oxford: Clarendon Press.

SEN, A. (1983). Poor, Relatively Speaking. *Oxford Economic Papers* 35 (2): 153-169.

SEN, A. (1985). *The Standard of Living*, Cambridge: Cambridge University Press.

SEN, A. (1992). *Inequality Reexamined*, Cambridge: Harvard University Press.

SEN, A. (1999). *Development as Freedom*, Oxford: Oxford University Press.

SLESNICK, D.T. (1993). Gaining Ground: Poverty in the Postwar United States. *Journal of Political Economy* 1010(1): 1-38.

SMITH, A. (1976). *An Inquiry into the Nature and Causes of the Wealth of Nations*, London: Methuen and Co.

SON, H.H. (2003a). Approaches to Defining and Measuring Pro-Poor Growth. Mimeo, World Bank, Washington D.C.

SON, H.H. (2003b). A note on pro-poor growth. *Economics Letters* 82(3): 307-314.

STEENBERGEN, M.R. AND B.S. JONES (2002). Modelling Multilevel Data Structures. *American Journal of Political Science* 46(1): 218-237.

STIGLITZ, J.E. (1976). The Efficiency Wage Hypothesis, Surplus Labor, and the Distribution of Labor in LDCs. *Oxford Economic Papers* 28(2): 185-207.

TAROZZI, A. (2004). Calculating comparable statistics from incomparable surveys, with an application to poverty in India. Mimeo, Duke University, Durham.

TEICHER, H. (1963). Identifiability of Finite Mixtures. *Annals of Mathematical Statistics* 34(4): 1265-1269.

TESLIUC, E. AND K. LINDERT (2004). Risk and Vulnerability in Guatemala: A Quantitative and Qualitative Assessment. *Social Protection Discussion Paper* 0404, World Bank, Washington D.C.

TOWNSEND, P. (1971). *The Concept of Poverty*, London: Heinemann.

TOWNSEND, R.M. (1994). Risk and Insurance in Village India. *Econometrica* 62(3): 539-591.

TOWNSEND, R.M. (1995). Consumption Insurance: An Evaluation of Risk-Bearing Systems in Low-Income Economies. *Journal of Economic Perspectives* 9(3): 83-102.

UDRY, C. (1995). Risk and Saving in Northern Nigeria. *The American Economic Review* 85(5): 1287-1300.

UNDP (2005). *Human Development Report 2005*, New York: Palgrave Macmillan.

UNITED NATIONS (2005). *The Millennium Development Goals Report*, New York: United Nations.

WATTS, H. (1968). An Economic Definition of Poverty. In: Moynihan, D.P. (ed.), *On Understanding Poverty*, New York: Basic Books.

WOOLARD, I. AND S. KLASEN (2005). Income Mobility and Household Poverty Dynamics in South Africa. *Journal of Development Studies* 41(5): 865-897.

WORLD BANK (2004). Burkina Faso: Reducing poverty through sustained equitable growth. Poverty Assessment. *Report* 29743-BUR, World Bank, Washington D.C.

WORLD BANK (2005). *World Development Report 2005*, World Bank, Washington D.C.

**Göttinger Studien zur Entwicklungsökonomik**
**Göttingen Studies in Development Economics**

Herausgegeben von/Edited by Hermann Sautter
und/and Stephan Klasen

Die Bände 1-8 sind über die Vervuert Verlagsgesellschaft (Frankfurt/M.) zu beziehen.

Bd./Vol. 9 Hermann Sautter / Rolf Schinke (eds.): Social Justice in a Market Economy. 2001.

Bd./Vol.10 Philipp Albert Theodor Kircher: Poverty Reduction Strategies. A comparative study applied to empirical research. 2002.

Bd./Vol.11 Matthias Blum: Weltmarktintegration, Wachstum und Innovationsverhalten in Schwellenländern. Eine theoretische Diskussion mit einer Fallstudie über „Argentinien 1990-1999". 2003.

Bd./Vol.12 Jan Müller-Scheeßel: Die Privatisierung und Regulierung des Wassersektors. Das Beispiel Buenos Aires/Argentinien. 2003.

Bd./Vol.13 Ludger J. Löning: Economic Growth, Biodiversity Conservation, and the Formation of Human Capital in a Developing Country. 2004.

Bd./Vol.14 Silke Woltermann: Transitions in Segmented Labor Markets. The Case of Brazil. 2004.

Bd./Vol.15 Jörg Stosberg: Political Risk and the Institutional Environment for Foreign Direct Investment in Latin America. An Empirical Analysis with a Case Study on Mexico. 2005.

Bd./Vol.16 Derk Bienen: Die politische Ökonomie von Arbeitsmarktreformen in Argentinien. 2005.

Bd./Vol.17 Dierk Herzer: Exportdiversifizierung und Wirtschaftswachstum. Das Fallbeispiel Chile. 2006.

Bd./Vol.18 Jann Lay: Poverty and Distributional Impact of Economic Policies and External Shocks. Three Case Studies from Latin America Combining Macro and Micro Approaches. 2007.

Bd./Vol.19 Kenneth Harttgen: Empirical Analysis of Determinants, Distribution and Dynamics of Poverty. 2007.

Bd./Vol. 20 Stephan Klasen / Felicitas Nowak-Lehmann: Poverty, Inequality and Migration in Latin America. 2007.

Bd./Vol. 21 Isabel Günther: Empirical Analysis of Poverty Dynamics. With Case Studies from Sub-Saharan Africa. 2007.

**Peter Lang · Internationaler Verlag der Wissenschaften**

Jann Lay

# Poverty and Distributional Impact of Economic Policies and External Shocks

## Three Case Studies from Latin America Combining Macro and Micro Approaches

Frankfurt am Main, Berlin, Bern, Bruxelles, New York, Oxford, Wien, 2007.
154 pp., num. fig., tab. and graph.
Göttingen Studies in Development Economics.
Edited by Hermann Sautter and Stephan Klasen. Vol. 18
ISBN 978-3-631-56559-9 · pb. € 34.–*

Economists have had much to say about the impact of economic policies on growth, but little on their distributional consequences and poverty impact. The reorientation of development policy from structural adjustment to poverty reduction as the central objective thus called for new tools to examine distributional change. This book analyzes the poverty and distributional impact of policy changes and external shocks in three case studies from Latin America: Trade liberalization in Colombia and Brazil, and the gas boom in Bolivia. It uses an innovative approach that combines computable general equilibrium and microsimulation models. The country applications illustrate that distributional consequences depend very much on the nature of the shock or policy change as well as the characteristics of the country in question. The book issues a warning against policy prescriptions being based on oversimplifying assumptions and models.

*Contents*: Poverty and distributional impact analysis · Country case studies from Latin America · Trade liberalization in Colombia · Doha-Round in Brazil · Bolivian gas boom · Combination of computable general equilibrium and microsimulation models · Sequential macro-micro models

Frankfurt am Main · Berlin · Bern · Bruxelles · New York · Oxford · Wien
Distribution: Verlag Peter Lang AG
Moosstr. 1, CH-2542 Pieterlen
Telefax 0041 (0) 32/376 17 27

*The €-price includes German tax rate
Prices are subject to change without notice

**Homepage http://www.peterlang.de**